Lindley Murray

Power of Religion on the Mind in Retirement, Affliction and at the Approach of Death

Lindley Murray

Power of Religion on the Mind in Retirement, Affliction and at the Approach of Death

ISBN/EAN: 9783337037291

Printed in Europe, USA, Canada, Australia, Japan

Cover: Foto ©Lupo / pixelio.de

More available books at **www.hansebooks.com**

THE POWER OF RELIGION

ON

THE MIND,

IN

RETIREMENT, AFFLICTION,

AND AT

THE APPROACH OF DEATH;

EXEMPLIFIED IN THE TESTIMONIES AND EXPERIENCE OF PERSONS
DISTINGUISHED BY THEIR GREATNESS, LEARNING, OR VIRTUE.

'Tis immortality,—'t is that alone,
Amidst Life's pains, abasements, emptiness,
The soul can comfort, elevate, and fill.—*Young.*

BY LINDLEY MURRAY,

AUTHOR OF AN ENGLISH GRAMMAR, &c. &c.

NEW YORK:

PRINTED BY ORDER OF THE TRUSTEES OF THE RESIDUARY
ESTATE OF LINDLEY MURRAY.
WILLIAM WOOD & CO., 61 WALKER STREET.
1868.

ADVERTISEMENT.

LINDLEY MURRAY, the author of this work, in his last
will, bequeathed certain funds to Trustees in America,
his native country, for several benevolent objects, among
which is the gratuitous distribution of "Books calculated
to promote piety and virtue and the truth of Christianity"
—and of which books he desired that "The Power of
Religion on the Mind" might form a considerable part.
NEW YORK, 1836.

The Life of James Gardiner has been omitted in this edition.

INTRODUCTION.

' To excite serious reflections on the unsatisfying and transitory nature of temporal enjoyments; and to promote a lively concern for the attainment of that felicity, which will be complete and permanent; are the objects of the present publication.

Piety and virtue, abstractedly considered, are truly amiable, and appear worthy of our earnest pursuit. But when recommended by the lives and testimonies of eminent persons, who have known the world, and experienced the emptiness of its honors, wealth, and pleasures, they derive additional importance; and constrain us to acknowledge, that the greatest happiness of man is to be found in religion.

Among the most important blessings, which the Divine Being has conferred upon mankind, may be numbered, the happy display of good and pious examples. In every age and country, perhaps in almost every little district throughout the earth, he has placed some of his faithful servants, or returning prodigals, to bear witness of his power and goodness, and to encourage others to a life of purity, piety, and beneficence.

The following pages exhibit a few of those striking

examples. In the quiet hour of reflection, they may contribute to arrest the careless and wandering; to animate the sincere and virtuous; and to alarm those who have rejected the most important truths, and who contemn the restraints of religion and virtue.

A number of our fellow-creatures, of different periods, countries, and conditions in life, standing on the confines of mortality, and bearing a uniform and undisguised testimony to the power and excellence of religion, presents a solemn and interesting spectacle. With the prospect of immortality before them, and no longer influenced by those concerns and passions which obscure the understanding and harden the heart, they must be supposed to view their objects through a proper medium, and to speak the language of truth and soberness.

May the important testimonies of these preachers of righteousness, lead us to just and seasonable reflections on the state of our own minds; and produce a reverent application to our heavenly Father, for the aid of his Holy Spirit, to enlighten and strengthen us, and to conduct us safely through the paths of life! May his gracious protection be afforded at the close of our day, when the shadows of the evening shall approach, the glittering vanities of the world be obscured, and all its friendships and resources be found unavailing!

Trials and discouragements may, indeed, be expected to assail us, in this state of being.—On surveying our past lives, we must all be conscious, that, in numerous instances, we have violated the Divine Law, and incurred the penalty due to our disobedience. And this view of our condition often occasions deep regret; and is sometimes apt to overwhelm the drooping and diffident mind.

But whatever may have been our deviations from the paths of rectitude, we are encouraged to ask, and to hope for mercy. The goodness of God has freely offered to pardon all our sins, and receive us into favor, if we sincerely repent, and unfeignedly believe in Jesus Christ the Saviour of the world. In the Revelation of his will to mankind, the great design, conspicuous throughout, is, to manifest his love and compassion towards our fallen race, and to accomplish our salvation. "His tender mercies are over all his works." "He taketh pleasure in those who hope in his mercy." "As a father pitieth his children, so the Lord pitieth them that fear him. For he knoweth our frame : he remembereth that we are dust." The blessed Redeemer "came into the world to save sinners—to seek and to save that which was lost." And, to increase our gratitude and trust, he has graciously assured us, that "there is joy in the presence of the angels of God, over one sinner that repenteth."—These, and many other passages in the Holy Scriptures, afford an abundant source of consolation and encouragement, to the truly humble and penitent believer in Christ. And when applied to the heart by Divine Grace, they produce in us a holy confidence and joy.

Though the love and mercies of God are great beyond expression, yet, for wise purposes, his children are not equally favored by him, on the bed of languishing and death. But they are all permitted to hope, that, when this awful period approaches, He will preserve them from being distressed with mournful retrospects on the past, or with gloomy apprehensions of the future: that redeeming love will calm their fears and disquietudes; sustain them under every conflict; and animate them with the prospect of being soon admitted into the mansions of eternal felicity.

ADVERTISEMENT.

In the latter editions of this work, the author has been solicitous to make it acceptable, not only to persons of mature years, but also to many in younger life. As the characters which it contains, exhibit a great variety of striking and animating views of piety and virtue, and strongly recommend the Christian religion in particular; he indulges a hope, that instructors of youth will deem it a suitable book to be read, occasionally, by the higher classes of their pupils. It is of great importance to impress young minds with favorable sentiments of virtue and goodness; and to convince them, by practical evidence, that religion affords the best support and enjoyment, in this life, and the only sure ground of happiness in the world to come.

To render the performance more instructive, as well as more interesting, the author has introduced into it many important moral sentiments, and many reflections of a religious nature, as well as a considerable portion of useful, biographical information. The introductory narratives relative to the subjects of the work, will, he presumes, be found intimately connected with its chief design. They gratify curiosity, respecting the general character of the persons whose solemn sentiments are exhibited; they confer additional importance on the testimonies in favor of religion; and they relieve the mind from the effect, which a succession of deeply serious matter would occasion.

CONTENTS.

1*

CHAPTER V.

CHAPTER VI.

CHAPTER VII.

CHAPTER VIII.

CHAPTER IX.

CHAPTER X.

THE POWER OF RELIGION.

CHAPTER I.

SECTION I.

THE PATRIARCH JOB.

This venerable patriarch was so eminent an instance of the power of religion on the mind, under the most trying afflictions, that a short account of him may properly introduce these memoirs.

In the first part of his days, this distinguished person was "the greatest of all the men of the East." His possessions were large; his family was numerous and flourishing; his own character was fair and blameless: yet this person it pleased God to visit with extraordinary reverses of fortune. He was robbed of his whole substance.

His sons and daughters all perished; and he himself, fallen from his high estate, childless and reduced to poverty, was smitten with sore disease. His friends came about him, seemingly with the purpose of administering comfort; but, from a harsh and ill-founded construction of the intention of Providence, in his disasters, they only added to his sorrows, by unjust upbraiding.

In distress so poignant, what was the temper of this good man? Fully persuaded that all blessings come from God, who has a right to withhold or distribute them, as he sees best, he piously exclaims: "The Lord gave, and the Lord hath taken away; blessed be the name of the Lord!"

To his other calamities, this domestic affliction was added, that his wife, who ought to have soothed and alleviated his sorrows, provoked his indignation, by an impious speech. What firmness and resignation are marked in his answer to her! "Thou speakest as one of the foolish women speaketh. What! shall we receive good at the hand of God, and shall we not receive evil?" Though he forcibly felt the deplorable condition to which he was reduced, and most pathetically described and bewailed it, yet no doubt of divine goodness, no murmur against Providence, was suffered to rise in his mind. "In all this Job sinned not with his lips, nor charged God foolishly."

At length, the goodness of that God whom he served, and who had secretly supported him under all his sufferings, broke forth upon him with increased energy; and, like a cheering sun dispersing the surrounding gloom, again gladdened his heart with returning peace and prosperity. His riches were restored to him twofold. The loss of his former children was repaired by a new offspring. His name became again renowned in the East; " and the latter end of Job was more blessed than the beginning."

SECTION II.

SOLOMON.

Solomon is one of the most interesting and extraordinary characters mentioned in the sacred Scriptures. The advice which this prince received from his father David, a short time before his decease, is very remarkable; and doubtless made a deep impression on his mind: "Thou, Solomon, my son, know thou the God of thy father; and serve him with a perfect heart, and with a willing mind: for the Lord searcheth all hearts. If thou seek him he will be found of thee: but if thou forsake him, he will cast thee off for ever."

This king having made a great and solemn offering to God, soon after his accession to the throne, the Lord was well pleased with his piety and zeal; and desired him to "ask what he should give him." Humbled under the sense of the goodness of God to him, and of his incapacity to govern so numerous a people, he declared that "he was but a little child:" and, instead of riches and honor, and length of days, he desired that God would bestow upon him wisdom and knowledge, that he might prudently and happily rule the nation over which he had placed him. This choice was so much approved by the Almighty, that he gave him a wise and understanding heart, and added riches and honor to the gift.

Solomon was directed by God to build him a temple at Jerusalem: and this order he faithfully executed. The prayer which he made at the dedication of this grand edifice, breathes the most devout and humble disposition, and the most ardent desire for the real happiness of his people. One can scarcely ever peruse it, without feeling a degree of the same pious ardor which pervaded and animated the breast of the royal supplicant on that solemn occasion. At this moment, he shone in his highest lustre: nor can we conceive any thing upon earth more dignified and majestic, than his deportment on the dedication of this sacred structure. We are compelled to revere the character of the monarch, who with such uncommon zeal, stood before his nobles, his princes, and his people, as a preacher of righteousness, and as a priest of the most high God.

This illustrious prince, however, at one period of his life, so far mistook the source of true happiness, as to flatter himself with the hope of great enjoyments from the world. He sought for and obtained all the means of pleasure ; but found himself, in the end, greatly disappointed. The result of this search and experiment, he gives us, in these memorable lines: "I said to my heart, I will prove thee with mirth; therefore enjoy pleasure: and, behold! this also is vanity. I made great works, built houses, planted vineyards, made gardens and orchards, and planted trees in them of all kinds of fruits. I procured servants and maidens; I gathered silver and gold, and the peculiar treasure of kings. I obtained men and women singers, and the delights of the sons of men, as musical instruments, and those of all sorts. So I was great, and increased more than all that were before me in Jerusalem: and whatever my eyes desired, I kept not from them; I withheld not my heart from any joy. Then I looked on the works which my hands had wrought; and, behold! all was vanity and vexation of spirit."

After this full persuasion, that real happiness was not to be found in sensual pleasure or worldly honors, he concludes with solemnly recommending piety and virtue, as the great objects for which we were brought into being; and which will not only yield the best enjoyments of life, but will support us in that day, when we must make up our final account. "Fear God, and keep his commandments. This is the whole duty of man. For God will bring every work into judgment, whether it be good or whether it be evil."

"When we reflect," says Dr. Blair, "on the character of him who delivered these sentiments, we cannot but admit that they deserve a serious

and attentive examination. For they are not the
declarations of a pedant, who, from an obscure
retirement, declaims against pleasures which he
never knew. They are not the invectives of a
discontented man, who takes revenge upon the
world by satirizing those enjoyments which he
sought in vain to obtain. They are the conclusions of a great and prosperous prince, who had
once given full scope to his desires; who was
thoroughly acquainted with life in its most flattering scenes: and who now, reviewing all that he
had enjoyed, delivers to us the result of long experience and tried wisdom.

SECTION III.

CYRUS.

Cyrus may justly be considered as the most accomplished prince that we read of in profane history. He was possessed of wisdom, moderation, magnanimity; a genius for forming, and prudence for executing, the greatest designs. Of this extraordinary person,' the Almighty said: "He is my shepherd, and shall perform all my pleasure:" and he was accordingly made use of as an eminent instrument to punish wicked nations, and to promote the Divine will respecting the children of Israel.

When this great prince perceived the approach of death, he ordered his children, and the chief officers of state, to be assembled around him. On this occasion, the influence of religion on his heart was very conspicuous. He solemnly thanked the Supreme Being for all the favors he had conferred upon him, through the course of his life; implored the same care and protection for his children, his country, and his friends; and declared his elder son, Cambyses, his successor, leaving the other several very considerable governments. He gave excellent instructions to both of them. He observed, that the chief strength and support of the throne, were not vast extent of country, number of forces, nor immense riches, but just veneration toward God, good understanding between brethren, and the acquisition of true and faithful friends.

"I conjure you, therefore," said he, "my dear children, in the name of Heaven, to respect and love one another, if you retain any desire to please me for the future. For I do not think you will judge me to have no existence, because you will not see me after my death. You have never yet seen my soul: you must, however, have known by its actions, that it really existed. Can you believe, that honors would still be paid to persons, whose bodies are now but ashes, if their souls had no longer any being or power? No, no, my sons; I could never believe that the soul lived only while in a mortal body, and died when separated from it. But if I mistake, and nothing of me shall remain after death, fear the Deity, who never dies, who sees all things, and whose power is infinite. Fear him; and let that fear prevent you from ever doing, or deliberating to do, anything contrary to religion and virtue. Next to him, fear mankind, and the ages to come. You cannot be buried in obscurity: you are exposed upon a grand theatre to the view of the world. If your actions are upright and benevolent, be assured they will augment your power and glory. With regard to my body, my sons, when life has forsaken it, inclose it neither in gold nor silver, nor in any other matter whatever. Restore it immediately to the earth."

Perceiving himself to be at the point of death, he concluded with these words: "Adieu, dear children! May your lives be happy! Carry my last remembrance to your mother. And you, my faithful friends, those absent as well as those that are present, receive this last farewell! May you live in peace!" After he had said this, he covered his face and died, greatly lamented by the nations over whom he had reigned.

SECTION IV.

CONFUCIUS.

Confucius, the celebrated Chinese philosopher, was born in the kingdom of Lou, 551 years before the Christian era. When a child, he had a grave and serious deportment, which gained him respect, and plainly foretold what he would one day be. But he was most distinguished by his unexampled and exalted piety. He honored his relations; he endeavored in all things to imitate his grandfather, who was then alive in China, and a very pious man: and it was observable that he never eat anything, but he prostrated himself upon the ground, and offered it first to the Supreme Lord of heaven.

One day, while he was a child, he heard his grandfather fetch a deep sigh; and going up to him with much reverence, "May I presume," said he, "without losing the respect I owe you, to inquire into the occasion of your grief? Perhaps you fear that your posterity will degenerate from your virtue, and dishonor you by their vices."

"What put this thought into your head," said the old man to him; "and where have you learned to speak after this manner?"

"From yourself," replied Confucius: "I attend diligently to you every time you speak; and I have often heard you say, that a son, who does not by his virtues support the glory of his ancestors, does not deserve to bear their name."

At twenty-three years of age, when he had gained a considerable knowledge of antiquity, and acquainted himself with the laws and customs of his country, he projected a scheme for a general reformation of manners. Wisely persuaded that the people could not be happy, so long as avarice, ambition, voluptuousness, and false policy, reigned among them, he thought it incumbent upon him to recommend a severe morality; and accordingly, he began to enforce temperance, justice, and other virtues; to inspire a contempt of riches, parade, and splendor; and to excite such an elevation of mind as would render men incapable of dissimulation and insincerity. In short, he used all the means he could think of, to redeem his countrymen from a life of pleasure to a life of reason.

He was everywhere known, and as universally beloved: his extensive learning and great wisdom, soon made him known; his integrity, and the splendor of his virtues, made him beloved. Kings were governed by his counsels, and the people reverenced him as a saint. The good effects of his example and admonitions were, however, but temporary. He lived in times when rebellion, wars, and tumults, raged throughout the empire. Men had little leisure, and less inclination, to listen to his philosophy; for, as we have observed, they were ambitious, avaricious, and voluptuous. Hence he often met with ill treatment and reproachful language; and it is said that conspiracies were formed against his life: to which may be added, that his neglect of his own pecuniary interest had reduced him to extreme poverty.

Some philosophers among his contemporaries were so affected with this sad state of things, that they retired into the mountains and deserts, thinking that happiness could nowhere be found but in seclusion from society. In vain they endeavored to persuade Confucius to follow their example:—" I am a man," said he, "and cannot separate myself from the society of men, and consort with beasts. Bad as the times are, I shall do all I can to recall men to virtue; for in virtue are all things. If mankind would but embrace it, and submit themselves to its discipline and laws, they would not want me or anybody else to instruct them. It is the duty of a teacher first to perfect himself, and then to perfect others. Human nature came to us from Heaven pure and without defect; but in process of time, ignorance, the passions, and evil examples corrupted it. Reformation consists in restoring it to its primitive beauties: to be perfect, we must reascend to the point from which we have fallen. Let us obey Heaven. Let our reason, and not our senses, be the rule of our conduct: for reason will teach us to think wisely, to speak prudently, and to behave ourselves worthily upon all occasions."

Confucius did not cease to travel about, and do all the good in his power. He gained many disciples, who became strongly attached both to his person and his doctrine. These he sent into different parts of the empire, to promote reformation of manners among the people. All his instructions were enforced by his own example. He was remarkable for his gravity and sobriety, his rigorous abstinence, his contempt of riches, and what are commonly called the goods of this life; for his continual attention and watchfulness over his actions; and, above all, for his unaffected modesty and humility.

He is said to have lived three years in retirement; and to have spent the latter part of his life in sorrow. A few days before his last illness, he told his disciples, with tears in his eyes, that he was overcome with grief at the sight of the disorders which prevailed in the empire: "The mountain," said he, "is fallen: the high machine is demolished, and the sages are all fled." His meaning was, that the edifice of perfection, which he had endeavored to raise, was entirely overthrown.

He began to languish from that time; and a few days before his death expressed himself thus: "The kings reject my maxims; and since I am no longer useful on the earth, I ought not to regret leaving it." After these words he fell into a lethargy; and, at the end of seven days, expired in the arms of his disciples, in the seventy-third year of his age.

Upon the first hearing of his death, the prince, who then reigned in the kingdom of Lou, could not refrain from tears; " God is not satisfied with me," cried he, " since he has taken away Confucius."

Wise and good men are indeed precious gifts, with which Heaven blesses the earth; and their worth is seldom justly appreciated till after their decease. Confucius was lamented by the whole empire. He was honored as a saint; and so high a veneration was entertained for his memory, that it will scarcely ever be effaced in those parts of the world.

SECTION V.

SOCRATES.

Socrates, the greatest of the ancient heathen philosophers, was born about 467 years before the Christian era. His sentiments and conduct were, in many respects, very excellent, and command our admiration. He was blessed with extraordinary talents, which were improved by all the learning that the age in which he lived could afford: and he appeared at Athens under the respectable character of a good citizen, a true philosopher, and a wise instructor.

Convinced that philosophy is valuable, not as it furnishes curious questions for the schools, but as it provides men with a law of life, Socrates censured his predecessors for spending all their time in abstruse researches into nature, and taking no pains to render themselves useful to mankind. His favorite maxim was, "Whatever is above us, does not concern us."

His great object in all his conferences and discourses, was, to lead men into an acquaintance with themselves; to convince them of their errors; to inspire them with the love of virtue; and to furnish them with useful moral instructions. In these benevolent labors he was indefatigable. He communicated his instructions not only when he was in the chair, and at set hours of discourse, but even in his amusements; when he was at his meals; in the camp or market; and, finally, when he was in prison: thus making every place a school of virtue.

Through his whole life, this good man discovered a mind superior to the attractions of wealth and power. Contrary to the general practice of the preceptors of his time, he instructed his pupils, without receiving from them any gratuity. He frequently refused rich presents. The chief men of Athens were his stewards: they sent him provisions, as they apprehended he wanted them. He took what his present necessities required, and returned the rest. Observing at a particular time, the numerous articles of luxury which were exposed to sale at Athens, he exclaimed: "How many things are here which I do not want!"

His intrepid virtue, and the severity with which he reproved vice, produced the hatred of men whose principles and conduct were the reverse of his own. He was maliciously accused of corrupting the youth, and of despising religion, and was, with singular injustice, condemned to die. Before the trial, his chief accuser sent him a private message, assuring him that if he would desist from censuring his conduct, the accusation should be withdrawn. But Socrates refused to comply with so degrading a condition; and, with his usual integrity, replied: " Whilst I live I will never disguise the truth, nor speak otherwise than my duty requires."

After the sentence was passed, he was sent to prison, where he lay in fetters thirty days. In this long interval, with the prospect of death continually before him, he did not cease to enjoy that profound tranquillity of mind which his friends had always admired in him. He entertained them with the same cheerful temper which he had ever manifested : and Crito observes, that the evening before his death, he slept as peacefully as at any other time.

On the day assigned for him to die, his friends repaired early to the prison. They found him, with his chains off, sitting by his wife, who held one of his children in her arms. As soon as she perceived them, she made the prison resound with her cries. Socrates, that the tranquillity of his last moments might not be disturbed by unavailing lamentations, requested that she might be conducted home. With the most frantic expressions of grief she left the prison.

An interesting conversation then passed between Socrates and his friends, which chiefly turned upon the immortality of the soul. In the course of this conversation, he expressed his disapprobation of the practice of suicide; and assured his friends that his chief support, in his present situation, was an expectation, though not unmixed with doubt, of a happy existence after death. "It would be inexcusable in me," said he, "to despise death, if I were not persuaded that it will conduct me into the presence of the gods, who are the most righteous governors, and into the society of just and good men: but I derive confidence from the hope that something of man remains after death: and that the condition of good men will then be much better than that of the bad."

Towards the close of the day, he retired into an adjoining apartment to bathe; his friends in the meantime, expressing to one another their grief at the prospect of losing so excellent a father, and being left to pass the rest of their days in the solitary state of orphans. After a short interval, during which he gave some necessary instructions to his domestics, and took his last leave of his children, the attendant of the prison informed him that the time for drinking the poison was come.

The executioner, though accustomed to such scenes, shed tears as he presented the fatal cup. Socrates received it without change of countenance, or the least degree of perturbation. Then offering up a prayer, that he might have a prosperous passage into the invisible world, with perfect composure he swallowed the poisonous draught. His friends around him burst into tears. Socrates alone remained unmoved. He upbraided their pusillanimity, and entreated them to exercise a manly constancy, worthy of the friends of virtue.

"What are you doing?" said he to them: "I wonder at you. O! what has become of your virtue? was it not for fear of their falling into these weaknesses that I sent away the women? I have always heard that we ought to die peaceably, and blessing the gods. Be at ease, I beg of you, and show more firmness and resolution."

He continued walking till the chilling operation of the hemlock obliged him to lie down upon his bed. After remaining a short time in this situation, he covered himself with his cloak, and expired. Such was the fate of the virtuous Socrates! "A story," says Cicero, "which I never read without tears."

It was not till some time after the death of this great man, that the people of Athens perceived their injustice, and began to repent of it. Their hatred being satisfied, their prejudices removed, and time having given them an opportunity for reflection, the notorious iniquity of the sentence appeared in all its horrors. Nothing was heard, throughout the city, but discourses in favor of Socrates. The Academy, the Lyceum, private houses, public walks, and market-places, seemed still to re-echo the sound of his loved voice.

"Here," said they, "he formed our youth, and taught our children to love their country, and to honor their parents. In this place, he gave us his

admirable lessons, and sometimes made us seasonable reproaches, to engage us more warmly in the
pursuit of virtue. Alas! how have we rewarded
him for those important services!" Athens was in
universal mourning and consternation. The schools
were shut up, and all exercises suspended. The
accusers were punished for the innocent blood they
had caused to be shed; and the regard and gratitude of the Athenians towards this excellent man
rose to the highest degree of veneration.

MANY other instances might have been given, of
heathens, who, by their actions and discourses, appear to have been under the influence of religion;
but, in paganism, we find light so mixed with dark-
ness, religion and truth so blended with supersti-
tion and error, that the minds of Christians will be
less edified by examples of this kind, than by those
which exhibit piety and virtue, enlightened by the
rays of the gospel, and animated by the assurance
it gives of a happy immortality: we shall therefore
confine ourselves, in the succeeding pages of this
work, to instances of the power of religion on the
minds of persons who have lived under the Christian dispensation.

It is, however, to the serious and benevolent
mind, a source of thankfulness, to believe that the
Divine Goodness extends itself towards the upright

in heart of every age and every country. All mankind are, indeed the children of one beneficent
Parent, who will judge them by the degree of
light, and the law, which it has pleased him to afford
them. But whilst we indulge this charitable sentiment, it behooves us who, as Christians, are distinguished by pre-eminent advantages, to improve
them faithfully, to the honor of the Great Giver,
the good of mankind, and the edification of our
own souls.

SECTION VI.

STEPHEN THE PROTOMARTYR.

THIS excellent man lived in the Apostolic age; and was remarkable for his faith, his wisdom, and an eminent portion of the Holy Spirit, which it had pleased God to bestow upon him. Devoted to the service of his Divine Master, and anxious to promote the eternal happiness of men, he labored fervently to extend the belief, and the blessings of the Gospel. These endeavors were rendered successful by the support of his Lord; who enabled him to confirm his Divine mission, by the miracles which he performed among the people.

But the pious exertions of this upright and benevolent man, for the happiness of others, could not secure him from the malice and opposition of his enemies, who were influenced by a far different spirit. When these adversaries of true religion found themselves unable to resist "the wisdom and the spirit by which Stephen spake," they suborned witnesses to declare falsehoods, and to charge him with blasphemy, before the council. On this occasion, his innocence, and the sustaining power of his Lord and Master, were eminently conspicu-

2*

ous; for whilst "they who sat in council looked steadfastly on him, they saw his face as it had been the face of an angel."

In a speech of great simplicity and energy, and which marked the undaunted firmness of his mind, he defended the sacred cause which he had espoused. He gave a concise, but comprehensive history of the dealings of God with the Jewish nation; and set forth their repeated provocations, disobedience, and ingratitude, and the unmerited goodness and mercy of their Divine Lawgiver; and concluded with observing, that they themselves had been the betrayers and murderers of the Just One, the Lord and Saviour of the world. This faithful remonstrance, instead of affecting them with humiliation and sorrow, for their heinous transgression, excited the bitterest resentment against this firm and zealous Christian. "They were cut to the heart, and gnashed on him with their teeth."

At this moment, Stephen was animated by an extraordinary interposition of Divine power. "Full of the Holy Spirit, he looked up steadfastly into heaven, and saw the glory of God, and Jesus standing on the right hand of God." This miraculous vision he communicated to the council and people; which so enraged these unhappy creatures, "that they stopped their ears, and ran upon him with one accord, and cast him out of the city, and stoned him."

Whilst they were employed in this murderous deed, the faith of Stephen remained unshaken. "He called upon God, and said, 'Lord Jesus, receive my spirit!'" Far from feeling the least resentment towards these violent and wicked men, "he kneeled down, and cried with a loud voice, 'Lord, lay not this sin to their charge!'" What a glorious triumph was this of religion, the pure and benign religion of Christ, over the passions of human nature, and the malevolence of evil spirits!

SECTION VII.

THE APOSTLE PAUL.

THIS eminent apostle is supposed to have been born about two years before our Saviour. He was a native of Tarsus, in Cilicia, and a Pharisee by profession. The strong powers of mind which he possessed, were greatly improved by education. His parents sent him early to Jerusalem, where he studied the law, at the feet of Gamaliel, a doctor of high reputation; under whose directions he made a great progress in his studies; and afterwards became very zealous for a strict observance of the law of Moses. But his zeal carried him to great excess. He persecuted the church of Christ in the most violent manner. He entered into the houses of the Christians, and drew out by force both men and women, loaded them with chains, and sent them to prison. He searched for them even in the Synagogues; where he caused them to be beaten with rods, and compelled them to blaspheme the name of Jesus Christ.

In the midst of this mad and destructive career, he was arrested by a miraculous appearance of that gracious Being, whose religion he wished to extirpate; and who addressed him in these alarming expressions: "I am Jesus of Nazareth, whom thou persecutest." Struck to the ground, and humbled under a deep sense of the enormity of his conduct, he cried out, "Lord, what wouldst thou have me to do?"

From this period, he became sincerely and earnestly devoted to the service of his Divine Redeemer; who, in his unsearchable wisdom and mercy, made him an eminent instrument in establishing his church among the Gentiles. The same zealous and ardent temper by which he had been distinguished when attached to Judaism, being now influenced and directed by Divine grace, was entirely converted to the holy purpose of propagating the gospel of peace and salvation.

In this most benevolent work, he was indefatigable. No labor or fatigue discouraged him: no enemies or danger appalled him. Having been assured of the mercy and forgiveness of his Lord, and animated by the sense of his love, and of the unmerited honor of being employed in his service, Paul devoted all his powers, and made every sacrifice, to promote the blessed cause in which he had engaged. He thought that he could never sufficiently serve a Master, who had been so gracious and bountiful to him.

The enmity of his open and secret opposers, the various distresses and afflictions he encountered, ʀerved only to increase the ardor of his pious pursuits. The strong faith with which he was endued, raised him above all temporal considerations. "We are (said he) troubled on every side, yet not distressed; we are perplexed, but not in despair; persecuted, but not forsaken; cast down, but not destroyed."—"I am filled with comfort, I am exceedingly joyful in all our tribulation."

Supported by Divine Grace and future prospects, he seems to have considered all the labors and sorrows of this life, but as a drop of the ocean, as a grain of sand on the seashore, compared with that exalted state of happiness which awaited him, and which would last for ever. "Our light affliction, (says he,) which is but for a moment, worketh for us a far more exceeding and eternal weight of glory."

The life and writings of this distinguised apostle, exhibit numerous instances of his humility, selfdenial, patience, resignation, and fortitude; of his love to God, and love to man. IIis epistles contain a clear display of the doctrines of Christianity, and an ample detail of its precepts. They have been read, with comfort and edification, by the truly pious, in every age of the Christian church.

The nature and design of this work, will not allow us to recite many of the interesting occurrences in the life of this Apostle. We have, however, in addition to those already mentioned, selected the following, as striking proofs of the power of religion on his mind.

After having long acted as the Apostle of the Gentiles, his mission called him to go to Jerusalem, where he knew that he was to encounter the utmost violence of his enemies. Just before he set sail, he called together the elders of his favorite church at Ephesus, and, in a pathetic speech, which does great honor to his character, gave them his last farewell. Deeply affected by their knowledge of the certain dangers to which he was exposing himself, the whole assembly was filled with distress, and melted into tears. The circumstances were such as might have conveyed dejection, even into a resolute mind; and would have totally overwhelmed the feeble. "They all wept sore, and fell on Paul's neck, and kissed him; sorrowing most of all for the words which he spoke, that they should see his face no more."

What were then the sentiments, what was the reply of this faithful servant of God? His firm and undaunted mind expressed itself in these words: "Behold, I go bound in the spirit, to Jerusalem, not knowing the things that shall befall me there; save that the Holy Spirit witnesseth in every city, saying, that bonds and afflictions abide me. But none of these things move me; neither count I my life dear to myself, so that I might finish my course with joy, and the ministry which I have received of the Lord Jesus, to testify the Gospel of the grace of God."

Here we perceive the language, and the spirit, of

a truly great and religious man. Such a man knows not what it is to shrink from danger, when conscience points out his path. In that path he will resolutely walk, let the consequences be what they may.

This was the magnanimous behavior of the Apostle, when he had persecution and distress full in view. Let us attend to his sentiments, when the time of his last sufferings approached, and observe the majesty, and the ease, with which he looked on death. "I am now ready to be offered, and the time of my departure is at hand. I have fought a good fight. I have finished my course. I have kept the faith. Henceforth there is laid up for me a crown of righteousness."

How many years of life does such a dying moment overbalance? Who would not choose, in this manner, to go off the stage, with such a song of triumph in his mouth, rather than prolong his existence, amidst cares and anxieties, and even amidst the honors and enjoyments of the world?

SECTION VIII.

IGNATIUS.

IGNATIUS, one of the ancient fathers of the church, was born in Syria, and brought up under the care of the Apostle John. About the year 67, he became bishop of Antioch. In this important station, he continued above forty years, both an honor and a safeguard to the Christian religion; undaunted in the midst of very tempestuous times, and unmoved with the prospect of suffering a cruel death. He taught men to think little of the present life; to value and love the good things to come; and never to be deterred from a course of piety and virtue, by the fear of any temporal evils whatever; to oppose only meekness to anger, humility to boasting, and prayers to curses and reproaches.

This excellent man was selected by the emperor Trajan, as a subject whose sufferings might be proper to inspire terror and discouragement in the hearts of the Christians at Rome. He was condemned to die for his faith in Christ; and ordered to be thrown amongst wild beasts, to be devoured by them. This cruel sentence, far from weakening his attachment to the great cause he had espoused, excited thankfulness of heart, that he had been counted worthy to suffer for the sake of religion. "I thank thee, O Lord," said he, "that thou hast condescended thus to honor me with thy love; and hast thought me worthy, with thy apostle Paul, to be bound in chains."

On his passage to Rome, he wrote a letter to his fellow Christians there, to prepare them to acquiesce in his sufferings, and to assist him with their prayers. "Pray for me," said he, "that God would give me both inward and outward strength, that I may not only say, but do well; that I may not only be called a Christian, but be found one."

Animated by the cheering prospect of the reward of his sufferings, he said: "Now, indeed, I begin to be a disciple; I weigh neither visible nor invisible things, in comparison of an interest in Jesus Christ."—With the utmost Christian fortitude, he met the wild beasts assigned for his destruction, and triumphed in death.

SECTION IX.

POLYCARP.

Polycarp, an eminent Christian father, was born in the reign of Nero. Ignatius recommended the church at Antioch to the care and superintendence of this zealous father; who appears to have been unwearied in his endeavors to preserve the peace of the church, and to promote piety and virtue amongst men.

During the persecution which raged at Smyrna, in the year 167, the distinguished character of Polycarp attracted the attention of the enemies of Christianity. The general outcry was, "Let Polycarp be sought for." When he was taken before the proconsul, he was solicited to reproach Christ, and save his life: but, with a holy indignation, he nobly replied: "Eighty and six years have I served Christ, who has never done me any injury: how then can I blaspheme my King and Saviour?"

When he was brought to the stake, the executioner offered, as usual, to nail him to it; but he said, "Let me alone as I am: He who has given me strength to come to the fire, will also give me patience to abide in it, without being fastened with nails."

Part of his last prayer, at his death, was as follows: "O God, the father of thy beloved son, Jesus Christ, by whom we have received the knowledge of thyself; O God of angels and powers, of every creature, and of all the just who live in thy presence; I thank thee, that thou hast graciously vouchsafed, this day and this hour, to allot me a portion amongst the number of martyrs. O Lord, receive me, and make me a companion of the saints in the resurrection, through the merits of our great High Priest, the Lord Jesus Christ. I praise and adore thee, through thy beloved Son, to whom, with thee, and thy Holy Spirit, be all honor and glory, both now and for ever. Amen."

SECTION X.

THE VENERABLE BEDE.

Bede, surnamed the *Venerable*, was born about the year 673, in the neighborhood of Weremouth, in the bishopric of Durham. Losing both his parents at the age of seven years, he was, by his relations, placed in the monastery of Weremouth. He was educated there, with much strictness; and it appears, that from his youth he was devoted to the service of religion. He was ordained deacon, in the nineteenth, and presbyter, in the thirtieth year of his age.

He applied himself entirely to the study of the Holy Scriptures, the instruction of disciples, the offices of public worship, and the composition of religious and literary works. He wrote on all the branches of knowledge then cultivated in Europe. In Greek and Hebrew he attained a skill, which was very uncommon in that barbarous age: and, by his instructions and example, he formed many scholars. He made all his attainments subservient to devotion. Sensible that it is by Divine Grace, rather than by our natural powers, or by learning, that the most profitable knowledge of the Scriptures is to be acquired, he united with his studies regular prayer to God, that he would bless and sanctify them.

Perhaps no person of his time acquired so distinguished and widely-extended a reputation, as Bede; a reputation too, entirely founded on the worth of his character, and the extent of his learning. The Roman Pontiff respected him so highly, that he gave him a cordial invitation to the metropolis of the church : but this he thought proper to decline. In the eyes of Bede the great world had no charms.

Of his numerous and important writings, the greatest and most popular was, his "English Ecclesiastical History." All the knowledge which we have of the early age of Christianity in this country, is derived from this production.— King Alfred so highly esteemed the work, that he translated it from the original Latin, into the Saxon language ; and, by this means, increased its celebrity.

The various merits of Bede acquire additional lustre, from the general ignorance and corruptions of the time in which he lived. Notwithstanding this disadvantage, he appears to have been a man of eminent virtue ; and to have possessed the happy association of learning with modesty, of devotion with liberality, and high reputation in the church with humility and moderation.

In the last sickness of this pious and learned man, he was afflicted with a difficulty of breathing, which continued about two weeks. His mind was, however, serene and cheerful; his affections were heavenly; and amidst all his infirmities, he continued daily to instruct his disciples. At this period, a great part of the night was spent in prayer and thanksgiving; and the first employment of the morning was, to ruminate on the Scriptures, and make supplication to God.

Amidst his bodily weakness, his mind was still so active, that he employed himself in writing on religious subjects. His translation of the gospel of St. John, was not completed till the day of his death. When, at last, he perceived that his end was drawing near, he met the solemn event with great composure and satisfaction. "If my Maker please, (said he,) who formed me out of nothing, I am willing to leave the world, and go to him."— "My soul desires to see Christ, my king, in his beauty." He then, with pious elevation of mind, sung, "glory to the Father, to the Son, and to the Holy Spirit;" and expired with such tranquillity and devotion, as greatly affected all who saw and heard him.

SECTION XI.

LOUIS IX., KING OF FRANCE.

Louis IX., styled St. Louis, succeeded to the crown of France, in the year 1226. This king possessed great wisdom, piety, and virtue. His reputation for candor and justice was so great, that the barons of England, as well as king Henry III. consented to make him umpire of the differences which subsisted between them. Fenelon says of this patriotic prince: "He was distinguished by the nobleness of his sentiments: he was without haughtiness, presumption, or severity. In every respect, he attended to the real interests of his country, of which he was as truly the father as the king."

An abhorrence of sin was so deeply impressed upon his mind, by a religious education, that he not only preserved it through the course of his life, but was zealous to inculcate it upon others. He was very solicitous that his children should be trained up in the fear and admonition of the Lord; and used to devote a considerable part of his time to their religious instruction. He often related to them the punishments which the pride, the avarice, and the debauchery of princes, brought upon themselves and their people.

In his last sickness, he earnestly exhorted Philip, his son and successor, firmly to adhere to religion, in his own private life and conduct, and zealously to promote it among his subjects. He also strongly recommended to him justice, moderation, and all the virtues becoming a sovereign and a Christian. He strictly enjoined him never to suffer any one, in his presence, to speak disrespectfully of the Almighty, or of those devoted to his service; or to utter a word, tending, in the smallest degree, to countenance a crime. "God," said he, "grant you grace, my son, to do his will continually; so that he may be glorified by your means, and that we may be with him after this life, and praise him eternally."

His dying advice to his daughter Isabella, queen of Navarre, was also very expressive of his zeal for the cause of religion, and his solicitude for the welfare of his children. He wrote to her as follows: "My dear daughter, I conjure you to love our Lord with all your might; for this is the foundation of all goodness. No one is so worthy to be loved. Well may we say: 'Lord, thou art our God, and our goods are nothing to thee.' It was the Lord who sent his Son upon earth, and delivered him over to death for our salvation. If you love him, my daughter, the advantage will be yours; and be assured that you can never love and serve him too much. He has well deserved that we should love him; for he first loved us. I wish you could comprehend what the Son of God has done for our redemption.

"My daughter, be very desirous to know how you may best please the Lord; and bestow all your care to avoid every thing that may displease him. But particularly, never be guilty of any deliberate sin, though it were to save your life. Take pleasure in hearing God reverently spoken of, both in sermons and in private conversation. Shun too familiar discourse, except with very virtuous persons. Obey, my daughter, your husband, your father, and your mother, in the Lord: you are bound to do so, both for their sakes, and for the sake of him who has commanded it. In what is contrary to the glory of God, you owe obedience to none.

"Endeavor, my daughter, to be an example of goodness to all who may see you, and to all who may hear of you. Be not too nice about dress: if you have too many clothes, give them away in charity. Beware also of having an excessive care of your furniture. Aspire after a disposition to do the will of God, purely for his sake, independently of the hope of reward, or the fear of punishment."

Thus did this prince teach his children; and thus did he live himself. He died in great tranquillity, in the year 1270.

SECTION XII.

POPE EUGENIUS.

Gabriel Condelmerius was raised to the Papal throne in the year 1431; and took the name of Eugenius IV. From a low condition of life, and through various gradations of office, he ascended to this dignity. Being much averse to a reformation of doctrine and manners, he met with great opposition from some of the clergy; but being of a determined spirit, he encountered every danger, rather than yield to his opponents. He was often reduced to painful and mortifying situations, and experienced so many vicissitudes of life, that he had ample proof of the vanity and instability of human greatness.

The reflection he is said to have made on his death-bed, is remarkable; and shows that, in his greatest elevation, he did not find that peace and true enjoyment of mind, which he had possessed in an humble and retired situation. Being attended by a company of monks, he turned his face towards them, and said, with a voice, interrupted by sighs: "Oh Gabriel! how much better would it have been for thee, and how much more would it have promoted thy soul's welfare, if thou hadst never been raised to the pontificate; but been content to lead a quiet and religious life in thy monastery!"

SECTION XIII.

CARDINAL BEAUFORT.

CARDINAL BEAUFORT was of royal extraction, the son of John of Gaunt, duke of Lancaster; and was commonly called the rich cardinal of Winchester. It is generally believed that he concerted the death of Humphrey, duke of Gloucester, which was attributed to poison. History informs us that he prevailed with the king to grant him letters of pardon for all offences contrary to the statutes then enacted in England.

The wise son of Sirach exclaims, "O Death, how bitter is the remembrance of thee, to a man who is at ease in his possessions!" Of the truth of this sentiment, we have a remarkable proof, in the last moments of this ambitious cardinal. When he was arrested in the midst of his career, and the terrors of death were marshalled in horrid array before him, he thus complained, and vented his afflicted soul to his weeping friends around him: "And must I then die? Will not all my riches save me? I could purchase the kingdom, if that would prolong my life. Alas! there is no bribing death. When my nephew, the duke of Bedford died, I thought my happiness, and my authority greatly increased: but the duke of Gloucester's death raised me in fancy to a level with kings; and I thought of nothing but accumulating still greater wealth, to enable me, at length, to purchase the triple crown. Alas! how are my hopes disappointed! Wherefore, oh, my friends! let me earnestly beseech you to pray for me, and recommend my departing soul to God." Thus died this unhappy cardinal, in the year 1447.

SECTION XIV.

CÆSAR BORGIA.

CÆSAR BORGIA, a natural son of Pope Alexander VI., was a man of such conduct and character, that Machiavel has thought fit to propose him, in his famous book called "The Prince," as an original and pattern to all princes, who would act the part of wise and politic tyrants. He was made a cardinal; but as this office imposed some restraints upon him, he soon determined to resign it, that he might have the greater scope for practising the excesses to which his natural ambition and cruelty prompted him; for cruel, as well as ambitious, he was in the highest degree.

After this, he was made duke of Valentinois, by Louis XII. of France. He experienced a variety of fortune; but displayed, on every occasion, the most consummate dexterity and finesse, and seemed prepared for all events. The reflections he made a short time before his death, (which happened in the year 1507,) show, however, that his policy was fined to the concerns of this life; and that he had not acted upon that wise and enlarged view of things, which becomes a being destined for immortality. "I had provided," said he, "in the course of my life, for every thing, except death; and now, alas! I am to die, although entirely unprepared."

CHAPTER II.

SECTION I.

CARDINAL WOLSEY.

Thomas Wolsey, a distinguished person in the reign of Henry VIII., was born in the year 1471; and it is said he was the son of a butcher at Ipswich. Being made chaplain to the king, he had great opportunities of gaining his favor; to obtain which he practised all the arts of obsequiousness. Having gradually acquired an entire ascendency over the mind of Henry, he successively obtained several bishoprics; and, at length, was made archbishop of York, lord high chancellor of England, and prime minister; and was, for several years, the arbiter of Europe.

The emperor Charles the Fifth, and the French king Francis the First, courted his interest, and loaded him with favors. As his revenues were immense, and his influence unbounded, his pride and ostentation were carried to the greatest height. He had eight hundred servants; amongst whom were nine or ten lords, fifteen knights, and forty esquires.

From this great height of power and splendor, he was suddenly precipitated into ruin. His ambition to be pope, his pride, his exactions, and his opposition to Henry's divorce, occasioned his disgrace. This sad reverse so affected his mind as to bring on a severe illness, which soon put a period to his days.

A short time before he left the world, the review of his life, and a consciousness of the misapplication of his time and talents, drew from him this sorrowful declaration: " Had I but served God as diligently as I have served the king, he would not have given me over in my grey hairs. But this is the just reward that I must receive for my incessant pains and study, not regarding my service to God, but only to my prince."

With these painful reflections this famous cardinal finished his course. He affords a memorable instance of the vanity and inconstancy of human things, both in his rise and fall; and a striking admonition to those who are abusing the talents and opportunities, which God has given them to promote his honor and the happiness of men.

SECTION II.

SIR JOHN MASON.

A STRONG testimony to the importance of religion, is given by Sir John Mason, who, though but 63 years old at his death, had flourished in the reign of four sovereigns, (Henry VIII., Edward VI., Mary, and Elizabeth,) had been privy-counsellor to them all, and an attentive observer of the various revolutions and vicissitudes of those times.

Towards his latter end, being on his death-bed, he spoke thus to those about him: "I have lived to see five sovereigns, and have been privy-counsellor to four of them. I have seen the most remarkable things in foreign parts, and have been present at most state transactions for the last thirty years: and I have learned, from the experience of so many years, that seriousness is the greatest wisdom, temperance the best physic, and a good conscience the best estate. And were I to live again, I would change the court for a cloister, my privy-counsellor's bustle for a hermit's retirement, and the whole life I have lived in the palace, for an hour's enjoyment of God in the chapel. All things now forsake me, except my God, my duty, and my prayers."

The chief field, both of the duty and of the improvement of man, lies in active life. By the graces and virtues which he exercises amidst his fellow-creatures, he is trained up for heaven. And since Divine Providence has established government and subordination amongst men, it follows, that high offices and stations of dignity, are compatible with true religion. It is, however, possible, that the minds of persons in authority, may be so much engaged with temporal concerns, as to leave little or no place for the higher duties of piety and devotion; duties which purify and exalt our nature, and give a proper direction and limitation to all our labors for the good of others.

From the regret expressed by Sir John Mason, it appears that his error consisted, not in having served his king and country, in the eminent stations in which he had been placed; but in having suffered his mind to be so much occupied with business, as to make him neglect, in some degree, the proper seasons of religious retirement, and the prime duties which he owed to his Creator.

SECTION III.

CHARLES V. EMPEROR OF GERMANY.

CHARLES V. emperor of Germany, king of Spain, and lord of the Netherlands, was born at Ghent, in the year 1500.

He is said to have fought sixty battles, in most of which he was victorious; to have obtained six triumphs, conquered four kingdoms, and to have added eight principalities to his dominions: an almost unparalleled instance of worldly prosperity, and the greatness of human glory.

But all these fruits of his ambition, and all the honors that attended him, could not yield true and solid satisfaction. Reflecting on the evils and mis-eries which he had occasioned, and convinced of the emptiness of earthly magnificence, he became disgusted with all the splendor that surrounded him; and thought it his duty to withdraw from it, and spend the rest of his days in religious retirement.

Accordingly, he voluntarily resigned all his dominions to his brother and son; and after taking an affectionate and last farewell of the latter, and of a numerous retinue of princes and nobility that respectfully attended him, he repaired to his chosen retreat. It was situated in Spain, in a vale of no great extent, watered by a small brook, and surrounded with rising grounds covered with lofty trees.

A deep sense of his frail condition and great imperfections, appears to have impressed his mind, in this extraordinary resolution, and through the remainder of his life. As soon as he landed in Spain, he fell prostrate on the ground, and considering himself now as dead to the world, he kissed the earth, and said; "Naked came I out of my mother's womb, and naked I now return to thee, thou common mother of mankind!"

In this humble retreat he spent his time in religious exercises, and innocent employments; and buried here, in solitude and silence, his grandeur, his ambition, together with all those vast projects, which, for near half a century, had alarmed and agitated Europe, and filled every kingdom in it, by turns, with the terror of his arms, and the dread of being subjected to his power. Far from taking any part in the political transactions of the world, he restrained his curiosity even from any inquiry concerning them; and seemed to view the busy scene he had abandoned, with an elevation and indifference of mind, which arose from his thorough experience of its vanity, as well as from the pleasing reflection of having disengaged himself from its cares and temptations.

Here he enjoyed more solid happiness, than all his grandeur had ever yielded him: as a full proof of which he has left this short, but comprehensive testimony: "I have tasted more satisfaction in my solitude, in one day, than in all the triumphs of my former reign. The sincere study, profession, and practice, of the Christian religion, have in them such joys and sweetness as are seldom found in courts and grandeur."

SECTION IV.

SIR THOMAS SMITH.

Sir Thomas Smith was born in the year 1514, and received a liberal and polished education. In 1542, he was made king's professor of civil law in the university of Cambridge, and chancellor of the diocess of Ely. He was several times employed by Queen Elizabeth as her ambassador to the court of France; and executed the high office of secretary of state to that princess. His abilities were excellent, and his attainments uncommonly great. He was a philosopher, a physician, a chemist, a mathematician, a linguist, a historian, and an architect.

This distinguished person, a short time before his decease, was much affected by the prospect of his dissolution, and of a future state. He sent to his friends, the bishops of Winchester and Worcester, and entreated them to state to him, from the Holy Scriptures, the plainest and surest way of making his peace with God: adding, " It is lamentable, that men consider not for what end they are born into the world, till they are ready to go out of it."

It is truly a sorrowful reflection, that the pursuits of this life, and the love of the world, are often so much indulged, as to captivate the mind, and charm it into a state of insensibility to the great end of its existence. How much wiser and happier should we be, if we engaged in temporal concerns with moderation and restraint, the true way to extract all their good, and considered ourselves as strangers and pilgrims travelling towards a better country; instead of being occupied, under continual anxiety and frequent disappointments, in the delusive chase of interest and pleasure, till the scene is nearly closed, and the mind left to the anguish of a melancholy retrospect!

The flood of time is fast approaching: it will soon pass over us, and bury in silence and oblivion, all our busy, fascinating schemes and engagements; and leave nothing to survive the wreck, but virtue and goodness, and the consciousness of Divine favor. What urgent motives for correcting our terrestrial aims and labors, and for striving to become heirs of that kingdom, whose honors and enjoyments are perfect, and will last for ever!

SECTION V.

BERNARD GILPIN.

Bernard Gilpin, a man of exalted virtue, and distinguished among his contemporaries by the title of *The Apostle of the North*, was born in the year 1517, and descended from a respectable family in Westmoreland.

As he early discovered much seriousness of disposition, and an inclination to a contemplative life, his parents determined to educate him to the church; and accordingly placed him in a grammar school, where he passed through the different classes with great approbation. When he was sixteen years of age, he was sent to the university of Oxford, and entered a scholar on the foundation of Queen's college. In this situation, he soon became distinguished for the diligence with which he applied to his academical studies; and for his proficiency in that knowledge, which the defective systems of education then existing afforded.

Of his great progress in the study of divinity, and of the Greek and Hebrew languages, his exercises and disputations in the public schools gave very satisfactory evidence, and recommended him to much notice in the university; where he was, at the same time, admired and loved for the sweetness of his disposition, and the simplicity and gentleness of his manners.

His attachment to the Roman Catholic religion, in which he had been educated, was, for some time, strong and decided. But, an honest and ardent desire to discover truth; an unprejudiced study of the Holy Scriptures; and frequent conferences with pious and learned men; produced, at length, a thorough persuasion of the truth of the Protestant reformed religion. This cause he steadily and zealously supported, through the whole remaining course of his life.

The chief place of Gilpin's active and virtuous exertions, was in the county of Durham. After having resigned several benefices, which the opposition of his enemies, and other circumstances, would not permit him to occupy with satisfaction, he accepted the rectory of Houghton-le-spring. This living was of considerable value; but the duty of it was proportionably laborious. It was so extensive, that it contained not fewer than fourteen villages. It had been much neglected; and in it there scarcely remained any traces of true Christianity.

Gilpin was grieved to see the ignorance and vice, which so greatly prevailed in the places under his care. But he did not despair of bringing into order a waste so miserably uncultivated: and, by resolution, diligence, prudence, and perseverance, he finally succeeded in producing an astonishing change, not only in the character and manners of his own parishioners, but of the savage inhabitants in other northern districts. On his arrival among them, the people crowded about him, and listened to his discourses with great attention, perceiving him to be a teacher of a very different kind from those to whom they had hitherto been accustomed; and by his truly pastoral and affectionate treatment of them, he quickly gained their confidence, respect, and attachment.

Gilpin had not been long settled at Houghton, before Bishop Tonstal was desirous of still farther improving his fortune, by presenting him to a vacant prebend in the cathedral of Durham. But, resolving not to accept it, he told the bishop that, "by his bounty, he had already more wealth than, he was afraid, he could give a good account of. He begged, therefore, that he might not have an additional charge; but rather that his lordship would bestow this preferment on one by whom it was more wanted."

In these perilous times, (the reign of the sanguinary Queen Mary,) his steady, though mild and temperate, adherence to the reformed religion, involved him in many dangers and difficulties; from which he was often happily extricated, under Divine Providence, by the favor of Bishop Tonstal, and by his own judicious conduct. The malice of

his enemies was probably increased by his unaffected piety, and exemplary life; which formed a
striking satire on their negligence and irregularities.
They determined, therefore, to remove, if possible,
so disagreeable a contrast, and so able a reformer.

After many unsuccessful attempts to disgrace
and destroy him, their hatred so far prevailed, that
they procured an order from the merciless Bon-
ner, bishop of London, to have him arrested and
brought to that city; where, the bishop declared,
he should be at the stake in a fortnight. Gilpin
was speedily apprised by his friends of the measures determined against him; and earnestly entreated to provide for his safety, by withdrawing
from the kingdom. But their persuasions were
ineffectual; for having been long preparing himself to suffer for the truth, he now determined not
to decline it. He therefore, with great composure,
waited for the arrival of the bishop's messengers,
after having ordered his servant to provide a long
garment for him, in which he might go decently to
the stake.

In a few days he was apprehended; but before
he reached London, an account of Queen Mary's
death was received; by which event he was delivered from any farther prosecution. Thus provi-
dentially rescued from his enemies, he returned to
Houghton through crowds of people, who expressed the utmost joy, and rendered thakns to
God for his deliverance.

On the accession of Elizabeth, he was offered the bishopric of Carlisle, but this he modestly and firmly declined to accept. Not long afterward, the provostship of Queen's college, Oxford, was tendered to him. This honor and emolument he likewise declined. He believed that he could be more useful, in his present charge at Houghton, than elsewhere : and this was a consideration superior to every other, in the mind of the pious and benevolent Gilpin.

Eminent as his labors and generosity were, he was still unsatisfied with the services he had rendered to his fellow-creatures : and therefore, to the surprise of his friends, he undertook to build and endow a grammar school ; a design which his great management and frugality enabled him to accomplish. The school began to flourish as soon as it was opened ; and there was so great a resort of young people to it, that in a little time the town was not able to accommodate them. Gilpin therefore fitted up a part of his own house for that purpose where he boarded twenty or thirty children ; and bestowed clothing and maintenance on the greater part of them, whose parents were in poor circumstances.

Gilpin's hospitable manner of living was the admiration of the whole country. Strangers and travellers found a cheerful reception at his board. He was also pleased with the company of men of worth and letters, who used much to frequent his house. When Lord Burleigh, then lord-treasurer, was sent by Queen Elizabeth to transact some affairs in Scotland, he could not resist the desire which he felt, on his return, to see a man whose name he found everywhere mentioned with the highest respect. He had not time to give any notice of his intended visit; but the economy of so plentiful a house was not easily disconcerted. Gilpin received his noble guest with so much true politeness; and treated him and his whole retinue in so affluent and generous a manner, that the treasurer often afterwards said, "he could hardly have expected more at Lambeth."

While Lord Burleigh stayed at Houghton, he took great pains to acquaint himself with the order and regularity with which every thing in that house was managed; and he was not a little pleased with the result of his enquiries. There too he saw true simplicity of manners; and every social virtue regulated by exact prudence. The statesman began to unbend; and he could scarcely avoid comparing, with a kind of envious eye, the unquiet scenes of vice and vanity in which he was engaged, with the calmness of this interesting retreat.

At length, with reluctance, he took his leave, embracing the worthy rector with all the warmth of affection, and the strongest assurances of his readiness to render him any services at court, or elsewhere. When he had mounted a hill about a mile from Houghton, and which commands the vale, he turned his horse to take one more view of the place; and having kept his eye fixed upon it for some time, he broke out into these exclamations: "There is the enjoyment of life indeed! Who can blame that man for not accepting a bishopric? What does he want to make him greater, or happier, or more useful to mankind?"

After the lapse of many years spent in the cheerful, but laborious discharge of duty, this pious man perceived, from his many infirmities, that his end was drawing near. He told his friends his apprehensions; and spoke of his death with that happy composure which usually attends the conclusion of a good life. He was soon after confined to his chamber. His understanding continued perfect to the last. Of the manner of his taking leave of the world, we have the following account:

A few days before his death, having ordered himself to be raised in his bed, he sent for the poor; and beckoning them to his bed-side, he told them he perceived that he was going out of the world. He trusted they would be his witnesses at the great day, that he had endeavored to do his duty among them; and he prayed God to remember them after he was gone. He would not have them weep for him. If ever he had told them any thing good, he would have them remember that in his stead. Above all things, he exhorted them to fear God, and keep his commandments; telling them, if they would do this, they could never be left comfortless.

He next ordered his scholars to be called in. To these, likewise, he made a short speech, reminding them, that this was their time, if they had any desire to qualify themselves for being of use in the world: that learning was well worth their attention, but that virtue was of much greater importance to them.

He next exhorted his servants: and then sent for several persons who had not profited by his advice, according to his wishes, and upon whom he imagined his dying words might have a better effect. His speech began to falter before he had finished his exhortations. The remaining hours of his life he spent in prayer, and in broken conversations with some select friends. He often mentioned the consolations of Christianity; declared that they were the only true ones; and that nothing else could bring a man peace at the last. He died in 1583, in the sixty-sixth year of his age.

In the preceding sketch of the life of this eminent Christian, and in the account of his death, we perceive the animating power of religion on his mind. The following faithful summary of his character, marks very conspicuously the happy influence of the same Divine principle; and exhibits to every reader a most instructive lesson.

The natural disposition of this worthy man was of a serious cast: yet among his particular friends he was uncommonly cheerful, sometimes facetious. His general behavior was very affable. His severity had no object but himself: to others he was gentle, candid, and indulgent. Never did virtue sit with greater ease on any one; had less moroseness; or could mix more agreeably with whatever was innocent in common life.

He had a most extraordinary skill in the art of managing a fortune. He considered himself barely as a steward for other people: and took care, therefore, that his own desires never exceeded what calm reason could justify. Extravagance was, with him, another word for injustice. Amidst all his business, he found leisure to look into his affairs; well knowing that frugality is the support of charity.

He was the most candid interpreter of the words and actions of others: where he plainly saw failings, he would make every possible allowance for them. He used to express a particular indignation at slander; often saying, "Slander, more than theft, deserves the gallows." He was remarkably guarded when he spoke of others: he considered common fame as a false medium, and a man's reputation as his most valuable property.

His sincerity was such as became his other virtues. He had the strictest regard to truth, of which his whole life was one consistent example. All little arts and sinister practices, those ingredients of worldly prudence, he disdained. His perseverance in so commendable a practice, in whatever difficulties it might at first involve him, raised his character, in the issue, above malice and envy; and gave him that weight and influence in every thing he undertook, which nothing but an approved sincerity can give.

Whatever his other virtues were, their lustre was greatly increased by his humility. To conquer religious pride, is one of the best effects of religion; an effect which his religion in the most striking manner produced.

With regard to his clerical office, no man could be more strongly influenced by a desire of discharging his duties. As soon as he undertook the care of a parish, it engrossed his attention. The pleasures of life he totally relinquished, and even restrained his favorite pursuits of literature. This was the more commendable in him, as he always had a strong inclination for retirement; and was often violently tempted to shut himself up in some university at home or abroad, and live there sequestered from the world. But his conscience corrected his inclination; as he thought the life of a mere recluse by no means agreeable to the active principles of Christianity. The very repose to which his age laid claim, he would not indulge; but, as long as he had strength sufficient, he persevered in the laborious discharge of the various duties of his station, and in the exercise of a most extensive charity.

In respect to his benevolence, it may justly be said, that no man had more disinterested views, or made the common good more the study of his life ; which was, indeed, the best comment on the great Christian principle of universal charity. He called nothing his own : there was nothing he could not readily part with for the service of others. In his charitable distributions, he had no measure but the bounds of his income, a small portion of which was always laid out on himself. Nor did he give as if he were granting a favor, but as if he were paying a debt : all obsequious service or acknowledgment, the generosity of his heart disdained.

No part of his character was more conspicuous than his piety. He thought religion was his principal concern : and, of course, made the attainment of just notions respecting it, his chief study. To what was matter of mere speculation, he paid little or no regard : such opinions only as influenced practice, he thought concerned him. He knew no other end of religion than a holy life : and therefore in all his enquiries about it, he considered himself as looking after truths, which were to influence his conduct, and make him a better man.

All his moral virtues became Christian ones: they were formed upon such motives, and they respected such ends, as Christianity approves and directs. It was his daily care to conform himself to the will of God ; upon whose providence he absolutely depended, in all conditions of life. He was resigned, easy, and cheerful, under whatever commonly reputed misfortunes he met with. Believing in a particular providence, he was grateful to Heaven for every benefit; and studied to improve religiously every afflictive event.

Such were the life and character of this distinguished person. A conduct so agreeable to the strictest rules of religion and morality, gained him, among his contemporaries, as was before observed, the title of the Northern Apostle. The parallel was indeed striking. His quitting the ancient doctrines, in the utmost reverence of which he had been educated; the persecutions he met with for the sake of his integrity; the danger he often ran of martyrdom; his contempt of the world; his unwearied application to the business of his calling; and the boldness and freedom with which he reproved the guilty, whatever their fortunes or stations were; might justly characterize him a truly apostolical person.

Viewed with such a life, how mean and contemptible do the idle amusements of the world appear! how trifling that uninterrupted succession of serious folly, which engages a great part of mankind, who crowd into a small compass every important concern of life! How much more nobly does that person act, who, unmoved by all that the world calls great and happy, can separate appearances from realities, and attend only to what is just and right; who, not content with the closest attainment of speculative virtue, maintains each

worthy resolution that he forms; and perseveres
steadily, like this excellent man, in the conscien-
tious discharge of the duties of that station, whatever it be, in which Providence has placed him!

This memoir is principally taken from a work entitled,
"The Life of Bernard Gilpin: by William Gilpin, M. A." It
is a valuable and interesting piece of biography.

SECTION VI.

JANE, QUEEN OF NAVARRE.

THIS excellent queen was the daughter of Henry II., king of Navarre, and of Margaret of Orleans, sister to Francis I., king of France. She was born in the year 1528.

From her childhood, she was carefully educated in the Protestant religion, to which she steadfastly adhered all her days. Bishop Burnet says of her: "That she both received the Reformation, and brought her subjects to it: that she not only reformed her court, but the whole principality, to such a degree, that the Golden Age seemed to have returned under her; or rather, Christianity appeared again with its primitive purity and lustre."

This illustrious queen, being invited to attend the nuptials of her son and the king of France's sister, fell a sacrifice to the cruel machinations of the French court, against the Protestant religion. The religious fortitude and genuine piety, with which she was endued, did not, however, desert her in this great conflict, and at the approach of death.

To some that were about her, near the conclusion of her time, she said: "I receive all this as from the hand of God, my most merciful Father: nor have I, during my extremity, feared to die, much less murmured against God for inflicting this chastisement upon me; knowing that whatsoever he does with me, he so orders it, that, in the end, it shall turn to my everlasting good."

When she saw her ladies and women weeping about her bed, she blamed them, saying: "Weep not for me, I pray you. God, by this sickness, calls me hence to enjoy a better life: and now I shall enter into the desired haven, towards which this frail vessel of mine has been a long time steering."

She expressed some concern for her children, as they would be deprived of her in their tender years; but added: "I doubt not that God himself will be their father and protector, as he has ever been mine in my greatest afflictions: I, therefore, commit them wholly to his government and fatherly care. I believe that Christ is my only Mediator and Saviour; and I look for salvation from no other. O my God! in thy good time, deliver me from the troubles of this present life, that I may attain to the felicity which thou hast promised to bestow upon me."

SECTION VII.

SIR FRANCIS WALSINGHAM.

SIR FRANCIS WALSINGHAM, an eminent person in the reign of Queen Elizabeth, was born at Chislehurst in Kent, of an ancient and honorable family. He made great progress in his studies at Cambridge: and, to complete his education, travelled into foreign countries, where he acquired various languages and great accomplishments.

He was three times sent ambassador to France. Queen Elizabeth made him Secretary of State, and employed him in the most important affairs. He had, indeed, a great share in promoting and accomplishing the extraordinary measures which distinguished that illustrious reign. It may be justly said, that he was one of the most refined politicians, and most penetrating statesmen, that are known in history. He had an admirable talent, both in discovering, and managing the secret recesses of the heart. To his sagacity and diligence, under Divine Providence, may be attributed the defeat of the king of Spain's grand Armada.

4*

This great man furnished a remarkable proof of his disinterestedness, and his preference of the public, to his private interest: for after all his eminent services to his country, he was so poor, that, excepting his library, which was a very fine one, he had scarcely effects enough to defray the expense of his funeral.

Some time before his death, which happened in 1590, he became deeply impressed with a sense of the superior importance of religion to all other considerations. In a letter to his fellow-secretary Burleigh, lord-treasurer of England, he writes thus: "We have lived enough to our country, our fortunes, our sovereign; it is high time to begin to live to ourselves, and to our God." This giving occasion for some facetious person of the court, to visit, and to try to divert him; he expressed himself to the following effect: "Ah! while we laugh, all things are serious around us. God is serious, who preserves us, and has patience towards us; Christ is serious who shed his blood for us; the Holy Spirit is serious when he strives with us; the whole creation is serious in serving God and us; all are serious in another world: how suitable then is it, for a man who has one foot in the grave to be serious! and how can he be gay and trifling?"

This enlightened and excellent person was, doubtless, friendly to a cheerful temper of mind, and to innocent recreations, on all suitable occasions: but he knew and felt, that there are events and circumstances in our lives, which call for peculiar circumspection and seriousness, as most congenial with our situation, and most conducive to our best interests.

SECTION VIII.

LADY JANE GREY.

This excellent personage was descended from the royal line of England, by both her parents. She was carefully educated in the principles of the Reformation. Besides the solid endowments of piety and virtue, she possessed the most engaging disposition, and the most accomplished parts. Being of an equal age with king Edward VI., she received her education with him, and seemed even to possess a greater facility in acquiring every part of manly and classical literature. She attained a knowledge of the Roman and Greek languages, as well as of several modern tongues; passed most of her time in application to learning; and expressed a great indifference for the occupations and amusements usual with persons of her sex and station.

Roger Ascham, tutor to the princess Elizabeth, having at one time paid her a visit, found her employed in reading Plato, while the rest of the family were engaged in a party of hunting in the park: and upon his admiring the singularity of her choice, she told him, that "she received more pleasure from that author, than others could reap from all their sports and gayety."

This amiable lady fell an innocent victim to the wild ambition of the duke of Northumberland; who, having effected a marriage between her and his son, Lord Guildford Dudley, raised her to the throne of England, in defiance of the rights of the princesses Mary and Elizabeth. At the time of her marriage, she was but eighteen years of age; and her husband was also very young.

Her heart, replete with the love of literature and serious studies, and with tenderness towards her husband, who was deserving of her affection, had never opened itself to the flattering allurements of ambition; and the information of her advancement to the throne, was by no means agreeable to her. She even refused to accept the crown; pleaded the superior right of the two princesses; expressed her dread of the consequences attending an enterprise so dangerous, not to say so criminal; and desired to remain in that private station in which she was born.

Overcome at last by the entreaties, rather than by the reasons, of her father and father-in-law, and, above all, of her husband, she submitted to their will, and was prevailed on to relinquish her own judgment. But her elevation was of very short continuance. The nation declared for Queen Mary: and Lady Jane Grey, after wearing the vain pageantry of a crown, during ten days, returned to a private life, with much more satisfaction than she could have felt when royalty was tendered to her.

Queen Mary, who appears to have been incapable of generosity or clemency, determined to remove every person from whom the least danger could be apprehended. Warning was, therefore, given to Lady Jane to prepare for death; a doom which she had expected, and which the innocence of her life, as well as the misfortunes to which she had been exposed, rendered no unwelcome news to her.

The queen's bigoted zeal, under color of tender mercy to the prisoner's soul, induced her to send priests, who molested her with perpetual disputation; and even a reprieve of three days was granted her, in hopes that she would be persuaded, during that time, to pay, by a timely conversion to popery, some regard to her eternal welfare.

Lady Jane had presence of mind, in those melancholy circumstances, not only to defend her religion by solid arguments, but also to write a letter to her sister, in the Greek language; in which she exhorted her to maintain, in every fortune, a like steady perseverance.

On the day of her execution, her husband, Lord Guildford, desired permission to see her; but she refused her consent, and sent him word, that the tenderness of their parting would overcome the fortitude of both, and would too much unbend their minds from that constancy, which their approaching end required. Their separation, she said, would be only for a moment; and they would soon rejoin each other in a scene where their affections would be for ever united, and where death, disappointments, and misfortunes, could no longer have access to them, or disturb their eternal felicity.

It had been intended to execute the Lady Jane and her husband on the same scaffold, at Tower-hill: but the council dreading the compassion of the people for their youth, beauty, innocence, and noble birth, changed their orders, and gave directions that they should be beheaded within the verge of the Tower. She saw her husband led to execution; and having given him from the window some token of her remembrance, waited with tranquillity till her own appointed hour should bring her to a like fate. She even saw his headless body carried back in a cart; and found herself more confirmed by the reports which she heard of the constancy of his end, than shaken by so tender and melancholy a spectacle.

Sir John Gage, constable of the Tower, when he led her to execution, desired her to bestow on him some small present, which he might keep as a perpetual memorial of her. She gave him her table-book, on which she had just written three sentences, on seeing her husband's dead body; one in Greek, another in Latin, a third in English. The purport of them was, that human justice was against his body, but that Divine Mercy would be favorable to his soul; that if her fault deserved punishment, her youth, at least, and her imprudence, were worthy of excuse; and that God and posterity, she trusted, would show her favor.

On the scaffold, she made a speech to the by-standers, in which the mildness of her disposition led her to take the blame entirely on herself, without uttering one complaint against the severity with which she had been treated. She said, that her offence was, not that she had laid her hand upon the crown, but that she had not rejected it with sufficient constancy: that she had erred less through ambition, than through reverence to her parents, whom she had been taught to respect and obey: that she willingly received death, as the only satisfaction which she could now make to the injured state: and though her infringement of the laws had been constrained, she would show, by her voluntary submission to their sentence, that she was desirous to atone for that disobedience, into which too much filial piety had betrayed her: that she had justly deserved this punishment, for being made the instrument, though the unwilling instrument, of the ambition of others: and that the story of her life, she hoped, might at least be useful, by proving that innocence of intention excuses not actions that any way tend to the destruction of the commonwealth.

After uttering these words, she caused herself to be disrobed by her women; and with a steady, serene countenance, submitted herself to the executioner.

We shall conclude the account of this virtuous and excellent young person, with a few remarks respecting her, made by bishop Burnet: " She read," says he, " the Scriptures much, and had attained great knowledge of religious subjects. But with all her advantages of birth and parts, she was so humble, so gentle and pious, that all people both admired and loved her. She had a mind wonderfully raised above the world ; and at the age, when others are but imbibing the notions of philosophy, she had attained the practice of the highest precepts of it.

" She was neither lifted up with the hope of a crown, nor cast down, when she saw her palace made afterwards her prison ; but maintained an equal temper of mind in those great inequalities of fortune, that so suddenly exalted and depressed her. All the passion which she expressed, was that which is of the noblest sort, and which is the indication of tender and generous natures, being much affected with the troubles which her husband and father suffered on her account. She rejoiced at her approaching end, since nothing could be to her more welcome, than to pass from this valley of misery, to that heavenly throne to which she was to be advanced."

SECTION IX.

SIR WALTER RALEIGH.

Sir Walter Raleigh, an illustrious Englishman, of an ancient family in Devonshire, was born in 1552. He was a man of admirable parts, extensive knowledge, undaunted resolution, and strict honor and honesty. As a soldier, a statesman, and a scholar, he was greatly distinguished; and was eminently useful to Queen Elizabeth, who protected and encouraged him in the various enterprises which he projected. He was the discoverer of Virginia; and took effectual measures for the settlement of the country, and for promoting its prosperity.

His active enterprises against the Spaniards, both in Europe and South America, excited the particular enmity of the court of Spain, which used every means to effect his destruction. During the reign of Elizabeth, these machinations were fruitless; but on the accession of James I., Sir Walter lost his interest at court, was stripped of his employments, and unjustly accused and condemned for a plot against the king.

He was afterwards trusted by James with a commission of considerable importance; and thus virtually pardoned for all supposed offences. The malice of his enemies, however, at length prevailed against him; and he was pusillanimously sacrificed to appease the Spaniards, who, whilst Raleigh lived, thought every part of their dominions in danger.

He was executed in Old Palace Yard, in the 66th year of his age. His behaviour on the scaffold was manly, unaffected, and even cheerful. Being asked by the executioner which way he would lay his head, he answered:—"So the heart be right, it is no matter which way the head lies."

During his imprisonment, and with the prospect of death before him, he wrote the following letters to his son, and to his wife. They contain many solemn and affecting admonitions: and testify the influence of religion on his mind.

In the letter to his son, he says: "My son, let my experienced advice, and fatherly instructions, sink deep into thy heart. Seek not riches basely, nor attain them by evil means. Destroy no man for his wealth, nor take any thing from the poor; for the cry thereof will pierce the heavens: and it is most detestable before God, and most dishonorable before worthy men, to wrest any thing from the needy and laboring soul. God will never prosper thee, if thou offendest therein. Use thy poor neighbors and tenants well. Have compassion on the poor and afflicted, and God will bless thee for it. Make not the hungry soul sorrowful: for if he curse thee in the bitterness of his soul, his prayer shall be heard of him that made him.

"Now, for the world, dear child, I know it too well to persuade thee to dive into the practices of it: rather stand upon thy guard against all those that tempt thee to it, or may practise upon thee, whether in thy conscience, thy reputation, or thy estate. Be assured that no man is wise or safe, but he that is honest. Serve God, let him be the author of all thy actions. Commend all thy endeavors to him, that must either wither or prosper them. Please him with prayer, lest if he frown, he confound all thy fortune and labor, like the drops of rain upon the sandy ground. So God direct thee in all thy ways, and fill thy heart with his grace!"

The following is a copy of the letter to his wife:

"You will receive, my dear wife, my last words, in these my last lines. My love I send you, which you may keep when I am dead; and my counsel, that you may remember it, when I am no more. I would not, with my will, present you sorrows, dear wife; let them go to the grave with me, and be buried in the dust: and seeing that it is not the will of God that I shall see you any more, bear my destruction patiently, and with a heart like yourself.

"First, I send you all the thanks which my heart can conceive, or my words express, for your many travails and cares for me; for though they have not taken effect, as you wished, yet my debt to you is not the less; but pay it I never shall in this world.

" Secondly, I beseech you, for the love you bear me living, that you do not hide yourself many days; but by your travails seek to help my miserable fortunes, and the right of your poor child: your mourning cannot avail me, who am but dust.

" Thirdly, you shall understand, that my lands were conveyed, *bona fide*, to my child: the writings were drawn at midsummer was a twelvemonth, as divers can witness. I trust my blood will quench their malice who desired my slaughter; and that they will not seek to kill you and yours with extreme poverty.

" To what friend to direct you, I know not; for all mine have left me in the true time of trial. Most sorry am I, that being surprised by death, I can leave you no better estate: God hath prevented all my determinations: that great God, who worketh all in all. If you can live free from want, care for no more; for the rest is but vanity.

" Love God, and begin betimes; in him you will find true and endless comfort: when you have travailed and wearied yourself with all sorts of worldly cogitations, you will sit down with sorrow in the end. Teach your son also to serve and fear God whilst he is young, that the fear of God may grow up in him: then will God be a husband to you, and a father to him; a husband and a father that can never be taken from you.

"Dear wife, I beseech you, for my soul's sake, pay all poor men. When I am dead, no doubt you will be much sought unto; for the world thinks I was very rich. Have a care of the fair pretences of men; for no greater misery can befall you in this life, than to become a prey unto the world, and afterwards to be despised. As for me, I am no more yours, nor you mine: death has cut us asunder, and God has divided me from the world, and you from me.

"Remember your poor child, for his father's sake, who loved you in his happiest estate. I sued for my life; but, God knows, it was for you and yours, that I desired it; for know it, my dear wife, your child is the child of a true man, who in his own respect despiseth death and his mis-shapen and ugly forms.

"I cannot write much: God knows how hardly I steal this time, when all are asleep: and it is also time for me to separate my thoughts from the world. Beg my dead body, which living was denied you; and either lay it in Sherborne, or in Exeter church, by my father and mother.

"I can say no more: time and death call me away. The everlasting God, powerful, infinite, and inscrutable, God Almighty, who is goodness itself, the true light and life, keep you and yours, and have mercy upon me, and forgive my persecutors and false accusers, and send us to meet in his glorious kingdom! My dear wife, farewell! bless my boy; pray for me; and may my true God hold you both in his arms!

" Yours that was, but not now mine own.

" WALTER RALEIGH."

SECTION X.

RICHARD HOOKER.

RICHARD HOOKER was born near Exeter, in the year 1553. He possessed great learning and sound judgment; and distinguished himself by a celebrated work, entitled, "The Laws of Ecclesiastical Polity." He was a meek and pious man, and spent his days in laboring to promote the glory of his Creator, and the happiness of men.

In 1585, he was made master of the Temple, which was deemed, by most persons, a noble preferment. But it was not so suitable to Hooker's temper, as the retirement of a living in the country; especially as he had to encounter much opposition. He therefore entreated the archbishop to remove him to a more peaceful residence.

"When I lost," said he, "the freedom of my cell which was my college, yet I found some degree of it in my quiet country parsonage. But I am weary of the noise and oppositions of this place: and, indeed, God and nature did not intend me for contentions, but for study and quietness."

His desire was, to be placed in a situation, "where," as he piously expresses himself, "I may see God's blessings spring out of the earth, and eat my own bread, in peace and privacy ; a place where I may, without disturbance, meditate on my approaching mortality, and on that great account, which all flesh must give at the last day, to the God of all spirits."

His exemplary and peaceable life did not, however, secure him from enemies, by whom he was grossly calumniated, and charged with conduct which he abhorred. Over these attacks, the good providence of God enabled him, at length, to triumph ; and his slanderers were convicted, and duly punished.

His grateful acknowledgments to Heaven, for this deliverance, were expressed in these terms :— "O my God! neither my life, nor my reputation, is safe in my own keeping; but in thine, who didst care for me, when I yet hung on my mother's breast. Blessed are they who put their trust in thee : for when false witnesses were risen up against me ; when shame was ready to cover my face ; when I was bowed down with a horrible dread, and went mourning all the day long ; then thou, O Lord, didst hear my complaint, pity my condition, and art now become my deliverer. As long as I live, I will magnify thy mercy, who didst not give me over to my enemies."

When his slanderers were about to be punished, he endeavored to procure their pardon : but finding his labors for this purpose fruitless, he observed, that "he would, however, pray, that God would give them repentance, and patience to undergo their punishment." After this deliverance, he was often heard to say: "O, with what quietness did I enjoy my soul, after I was free from the fears of this slander! And how much more, after the conflict with myself, and the victory over my desires of revenge!"

Hooker was not happy in his marriage: but he endeavored to profit by this trial, and to be cheerfully resigned to the will of God. To a friend, who expressed his sorrow for the troubles in which he saw him involved, he humbly replied in this manner: "My dear friend, I ought not to repine at what my wise Creator hath allotted for me : but I ought to labor, as indeed I do daily, to submit to his will, and to possess my soul in patience and peace."

A short time before his death, this humble and truly good man, expressed himself as follows: "I have lived to see that this world is full of perturbations; and I have been long preparing to leave it, and gathering comfort for the awful hour of making up my account with God, which I now apprehend to be near. And though I have, by his grace, loved him in my youth, and feared him in my age, and labored to have a conscience void of offence towards him, and towards all men; yet, if thou, Lord, shouldst be extreme to mark what I have done amiss, how shall I abide it? Where I have failed, Lord, show mercy to me; for I plead not my righteousness, but the forgiveness of my unrighteousness, through His merits, who died to purchase pardon for penitent sinners. And since I owe thee a death, Lord, let it not be terrible, and then choose thy own time; I submit to it. Let not mine, O Lord, but thy will be done!"

At another time he said: "God hath heard my daily petition: for I am at peace with all men, and he is at peace with me. From this blessed assurance, I feel that inward joy, which the world can neither give, nor take from me. My conscience beareth me this witness; and this witness makes the thoughts of death joyful. I could wish to live to do the church more service; but I cannot hope it; for my days are past, as a shadow that returns not."

Soon after he had uttered these expressions, his spirits failed him; and a short conflict put a period to his life, in the 47th year of his age.

CHAPTER III.

SECTION I.

SIR PHILIP SIDNEY.

Sir Philip Sidney was born in Kent, in the year 1554. He possessed shining talents; was well educated; and at the early age of twenty-one, was sent by Queen Elizabeth, as her ambassador to the emperor of Germany. He is described by the writers of that age, as the finest model of an accomplished gentleman that could be formed, even in imagination.

An amiable disposition, elegant erudition, and polite conversation, rendered him the ornament and delight of the English court. Lord Brooke so highly valued his friendship, that he directed to be inserted as part of his epitaph, "Here lies Sir Philip Sidney's friend." His fame was so widely spread, that if he had chosen it, he might have obtained the crown of Poland.

But the glory of this Marcellus of the English nation, was of short duration. He was wounded at the battle of Zutphen, and carried to Arnheim, where, after languishing about three weeks, he died, in the 32d year of his age.

This accomplished person, at the solemn period of approaching death, when a just estimate of things is formed, and when the mind looks round for support and consolation, perceived that the greatest worldly honors are only splendid vanities, and have but a momentary duration. At this period, he was so dissatisfied with his "Arcadia," a romantic work, ill agreeing with his present serious views of things, that it is said, he desired it might never be published.

After he had received the fatal wound, and was brought into a tent, he piously raised his eyes towards heaven, and acknowledged the hand of God in this event. He confessed himself to be a sinner, and returned thanks to God, that "he had not struck him with death at once; but gave him space to seek repentance and reconciliation."

Compared with his present views of religion, his former virtues seemed to be nothing. When it was observed to him, that good men, in the time of great affliction, found comfort and support, in the recollection of those parts of their lives, in which they had glorified God; he humbly replied: "It is not so with me. I have no comfort that way. All things in my former life have been vain."

On being asked, whether he did not desire life, merely to have it in his power to glorify God, he answered: "I have vowed my life unto God; and if he cut me off, and suffer me to live no longer, I shall glorify him, and give up myself to his service."

The nearer death approached, the more his consolation and hopes increased. A short time before his dissolution, he lifted up his eyes and hands, and uttered these words: "I would not change my joy for the empire of the world."

His advice and observations, on taking the last leave of his deeply afflicted brother, are worthy of remembrance. They appear to have been expressed with great seriousness and composure. "Love my memory; cherish my friends. Their fidelity to me may assure you that they are honest. But, above all, govern your wills and affections, by the will and word of your Creator. In me, behold the end of the world, and all its vanities."

SECTION II.

SIR CHRISTOPHER HATTON.

Sir Christopher Hatton possessed great abilities, highly cultivated by study and business. He was remarkable for his eloquence and powers of persuasion. Queen Elizabeth, by whom he was greatly esteemed and favored, made him lord high chancellor of England. And it was remarkable, that though he had never followed the profession of the law, his knowledge of it was so profound, that none of his decisions, as chancellor, were ever found deficient either in equity or judgment.

This learned man had a high veneration for the Holy Scriptures; and a short time before his death, particularly recommended to his relations, to search them seriously and diligently, in order to discover the will of God. "It is," said he, "justly accounted a piece of excellent knowledge, to understand the law of the land, and the customs of our country; but how much more excellent is it, to know the statutes of heaven, and the laws of eternity, the immutable and perpetual laws of justice and righteousness! to know the will and pleasure of the great Monarch and universal King of the world! 'I have

seen an end of all perfection; but thy commandments, O God! are exceedingly broad.'"

The knowledge of the Divine will, is, indeed, the
most important of all knowledge. Were we possessed of the most comprehensive understanding,
the finest imagination, and the most capacious
memory; were we able to penetrate into all the
secrets of nature, and sound the depths of every
art and science; and yet remain ignorant of, or
disregard, Him who is the Author of our being
and the Preserver of our lives, our Sovereign and
our Judge; we should, with a great deal of knowledge, mistake our highest interests, and be miserable for ever.

SECTION III.

LORD BACON.

Francis Bacon, viscount St. Albans, and lord high chancellor of England, was born in the year 1561. The following account of this celebrated philosopher, is taken from Addison:

"Sir Francis Bacon was a man who, for greatness of genius, and compass of knowledge, did honor to his age and country; I could almost say, to human nature itself. He possessed at once all those extraordinary talents, which were divided amongst the greatest authors of antiquity. He had the sound, distinct, comprehensive knowledge of Aristotle, with all the beautiful lights, graces, and embellishments of Cicero. One does not know which to admire most in his writings, the strength of reason, the force of style, or the brightness of imagination.

"I was infinitely pleased to find, among the works of this extraordinary man, a prayer of his own composing; which, for its elevation of thought, and greatness of expression, seems rather the devotion of an angel than of a man. His principal fault appears to have been, the excess of that virtue

5*

which covers a multitude of faults. This betrayed him to so great an indulgence towards his servants, who made a corrupt use of it, that it stripped him of those riches and honors, which a long series of merits had heaped upon him. But in this prayer, at the same time that we find him prostrating himself before the great mercy-seat, and humbled under afflictions, which at that time lay heavy upon him, we see him supported by the sense of his integrity, his zeal, his devotion, and his love of mankind; which gave him a much higher figure, in the minds of thinking men, than that greatness had done from which he was fallen. I shall write down the prayer itself, as it was found among his lordship's papers, written with his own hand:—

" 'Most gracious Lord God, my merciful Father! my Creator, my Redeemer, my Comforter! thóu soundest and searchest the depths and secrets of all hearts; thou acknowledgest the upright; thou judgest the hypocrite; vanity and crooked ways cannot be hid from thee.

" 'Remember, O Lord, how thy servant ˗has walked before thee; remember what I have first sought, and what has been principal in my intentions. I have loved thy assemblies; I have mourned for the divisions of thy church; I have delighted in the brightness of thy sanctuary; I have ever prayed unto thee, that the vine which thy right hand hath planted in this nation, might have the former and the latter rain; and that it might stretch its branches to the seas, and to the floods. The state and bread of the poor and oppressed have been precious in my eyes; I have hated all cruelty and hardness of heart; I have, though a despised weed, endeavored to procure the good of all men. If any have been my enemies, I thought not of them, neither has the sun gone down upon my displeasure: but I have been as a dove, free from superfluity of maliciousness. Thy creatures have been my books, but thy Scriptures much more so. I have sought thee in the courts, the fields, and the gardens; but I have found thee in thy temples.

"'Thousands have been my sins, and ten thousands my transgressions: but thy sanctifications have remained with me, and my heart, through thy grace, hath been an unquenched coal upon thine altar.

"'O Lord, my strength! I have, from my youth, met with thee in all my ways; in thy fatherly compassions, in thy merciful chastisements, and in thy most visible providences. As thy favors have increased upon me, so have thy corrections; as my worldly blessings were exalted, so secret darts from thee have pierced me; and when I have ascended before men, I have descended in humiliation before thee. And now, when I have been thinking most of place and honor, thy hand is heavy upon me, and has humbled me according to thy former loving-kindness, keeping me still in thy fatherly school, not as a bastard, but as a child. Just are thy judgments upon me for my sins, which are more in number than the sands of the sea, but which have no proportion to thy mercies. Besides my innumerable sins, I confess before thee, that I am debtor to thee for the gracious talents of thy gifts and graces; which I have neither put into a napkin, nor placed, as I ought, with exchangers, where it might have made best profit; but I have misspent it in things for which I was least fit: so I may truly say, my soul has been a stranger in the course of my pilgrimage. Be merciful unto me, O Lord, for my Saviour's sake, and receive me into thy bosom, or guide me in thy ways.' "

SECTION IV.

SIR HENRY WOTTON.

Sir Henry Wotton, an Englishman, eminent for learning, and for knowledge in state affairs, was born in the year 1568. He was often employed by James the First, as ambassador to several of the European states; and discharged the trust reposed in him, with ability, and to the satisfaction of the king. He enjoyed the favor of this prince, and was much esteemed and admired by his contemporaries. But these honors did not afford him that satisfaction which a wise man wishes to obtain. Amidst them all he could say: "It is the greatest happiness of my life, to be at leisure to be, and to do good."

Though he was much esteemed for his wisdom and regular deportment, yet near the end of his days, when he reflected seriously on his past life, he felt great concern; and often repeated these solemn expressions: "How much have I to repent of, and how little time to do it in!"

SECTION V.

PETER DU MOULIN.

Peter du Moulin, an eminent Protestant minister in France, was born in the year 1568. Bayle calls him "one of the most celebrated ministers, that the reformed church in France ever had to boast of." He was a man of such eminence, that James the First of England employed him to attempt the accomplishment of a union between the reformed and Lutheran churches.

This pious and excellent man was remarkable through life, for a low opinion of himself, and an unwearied diligence in doing good. In his last sickness, his meekness and humility were particularly prevalent. On hearing himself praised by one who thought he undervalued himself, he said, with indignation, "Away with this flattery, and pray to God to have mercy on me." "Lord," said he, "I have deserved nothing but punishment. Thou hast heaped blessings upon me. Thou hast honored me with a holy calling: but I have not labored according to the worth of it: I have mingled my own glory with thine. I have often neglected thy service, to seek my particular interest.

O, how much self-love! what perverseness has opposed the kingdom of thy Son within me! How often have I grieved thy Holy Spirit, by idle thoughts and carnal affections! and yet thou hast always shown thyself a gracious and merciful Father to me. Thou hast, indeed, sometimes chastened me with thy rod. Thou hast hid thy face from me for a moment: but thou hast remembered me in thy great compassion. Lord, thou art faithful in thy promises. I am thy creature. Thou hast led me, and taught me, from my youth: O forsake me not in this last period of my life."

To a person who commended his service, in the cause of religion, he replied: " Ah, my friend, you know not how much you grieve me by such language. I have not done all the good I ought to have done; and that little benefit which the church has reaped by my labors, is not from me, but from the grace of God which is in me; as he frequently produces a good effect with a weak instrument. I am conscious that I have neglected my duty in many things, and offended my God; but I have loved his holy truth, and I hope in his mercy."

His sickness was an inflammation of the lungs, with an ague, which returned with double violence every day at the same hour. Recovering from one of these fits, he said: "My God, how weary am I! When shall I rest in thy bosom? When shall I drink of the river of thy pleasures? I am unworthy of it, O my God! but thou art glorified by doing good to the unworthy. It is not for them who are whole, but for those who are sick, that thy Son, the great Physician, was sent."

A little before his death, waking about midnight, he said to a person who attended him, "I shall now soon be relieved. I am going to my Father and my God. He has heard me indeed. I go to him with confidence; for he has arrayed me with the robe of his righteousness." Soon after this, he gently expired; and his countenance retained the expression of joy.

SECTION VI.

DR. DONNE.

John Donne, an excellent English poet, was born in the year 1573. He was educated in his father's house till the eleventh year of his age, when he was sent to the university of Oxford; where it was observed of him, that "he was rather born wise, than made so by study." He travelled through Italy and Spain; where he made many useful observations, and became well acquainted with the languages of those countries.

After his return to England, he was solicited to go into orders, and to accept of a benefice; but at first, he prudently declined this offer for several reasons; chiefly, "because some former irregularities of his life had been too notorious not to expose him to the censure of the world; and would, perhaps, bring dishonor upon the sacred function." He was, however, strenuously urged by King James the First, with whom he was a great favorite, to enter into the clerical office: and after having maturely weighed the subject and employed a considerable time in improving himself by close study, he complied with the king's desire. He was ordained deacon and priest by the bishop of London; and soon after was appointed one of the king's chaplains. On the royal recommendation, he was presented with the degree of Doctor of Divinity, by the university of Cambridge.

Dr. Donne moved in a large circle of friends and acquaintance. He was much visited and caressed by the nobility, foreign ministers, and other persons of distinction. So generally was he beloved and esteemed, that, within the first year of entering into orders, he received offers of fourteen different benefices, from persons of rank. He preferred, however, settling in London; and was made preacher of Lincoln's Inn. About this time, his domestic happiness suffered a severe shock, by the death of a beloved wife, who left him with a young family of seven children.

Some years after this event, he had a dangerous illness; which gave occasion to a work entitled, "Devotions upon Emergent Occasions;" in which the fervor of his soul is strongly expressed. He recovered from this indisposition; and lived in good health, till he was seized with a fever in 1630, after which he began to decline. Foreseeing his end, he prepared for it with great resignation. He was, however, much affected with the retrospect of life: and on his death-bed, upon taking a solemn leave of his friends, he made this striking declaration to them: "I repent of all my life, except that part of it, which I spent in communion with God, and in doing good."

SECTION VII.

PHILIP III. KING OF SPAIN.

Philip the Third was born in the year 1577, and succeeded to the crown of Spain in the 21st year of his age. Of an inactive disposition, and averse to the trouble of governing a great kingdom, he committed the whole administration of affairs to his minister and favorite: and this was the source of many calamities to his subjects, and of perplexity and distress to himself.

When this king drew near the end of his days, he desired, as the last action of his life, to see, and to bless his children. He told the prince, his successor, he had sent for him, " that he might behold the vanity of crowns and tiaras, and learn to prepare for eternity." He kindly addressed all his children, gave them his blessing, and dismissed them with fervent prayers for their happiness, both here and hereafter.

During the progress of his disorder, he appeared to be greatly disturbed in mind. He made repeated confessions of his sins, and implored Divine mercy. He said to those around him, that he had often been guilty of dissimulation in matters of government. He deeply regretted his indolence, and blamed himself much for having devolved the cares of the state on his ministers. When he reflected, that he had not, in all things, made the will of God the rule of his government, he trembled, crying out at different times: " Oh! if it should please heaven to prolong my life, how different from the past should be my future conduct!"

Though the retrospect of his life filled his mind with bitter regret, and painful apprehensions, he expressed a hope that, through the merits of the Redeemer, he should at last be received into the mansions of the blessed. The affecting expressions of his repentance and devotion, drew tears from the eyes of those who surrounded him. The priest who attended him, unwilling to bruise a broken reed, endeavored to cheer and compose his troubled mind, by consolatory views of the Divine mercy, and the assurances which the Gospel affords, of assistance to the weak, and of pardon to the penitent. At length, the alternate tumult of hope and fear, which had so greatly agitated his mind, subsided into a gentle calm; and he died peacefully, in the forty-third year of his life and the twenty-third of his reign.

SECTION VIII.

CATHARINE BRETTERG.

CATHARINE BRETTERG was born in Cheshire, about the year 1580, and was the daughter of John Bruen, Esq., of Bruen Stapleford. From a child, she was much employed in reading the Holy Scrip. tures, which she found of great use and comfort to her She was moderate and sober in the enjoyment of the good things of this life; and carefully avoided the vain pleasures and fashions, in which many greatly delight themselves. The society of religious people was very comfortable and pleasant to her; and it appears that, from her childhood to the end of her days, she was concerned to live in the fear of God, and to walk before him with a perfect heart.

This excellent woman, in the beginning of her last sickness, was permitted to labor under great exercise and conflict of spirit: but she was mercifully supported under this trial; and the victory was, in due time, graciously given to her.

Her dependence on the Fountain of Wisdom and Strength, for relief from this trying state of mind, is evidenced by the following pious and fervent prayer: "O Lord God of my salvation, help my weakness; plead thou my cause, O God of Truth, for in thee do I trust! O blessed Saviour, perfect the work, I humbly beseech thee, which thou hast begun in me."

At another time, after she had experienced deliverance from this conflict, she expressed herself in the following manner: "Oh, my God, blessed be thy name for evermore, who hast shown me the path of life. Thou didst, O Lord, hide thy face from me for a little season, but with everlasting mercy thou hast had compassion on me. And now, blessed Lord,. thy comforting presence is come; yea, Lord, thou hast had respect to thy handmaid, and art come with fulness of joy and abundance of consolation."

When she was near her end, her strength and voice being very feeble, she lifted up her eyes, and with a sweet countenance, and still voice, said: "My warfare is accomplished, and my iniquities are pardoned. Lord, whom have I in heaven but thee? And I have none on earth besides thee. My flesh faileth, and my heart also; but God is the strength of my heart, and my portion for ever. He that preserveth Jacob, and defendeth Israel, is my God, and will guide me unto death. Direct me, O Lord my God, and keep my soul in safety."

Soon after she had expressed these words, she yielded up her soul in peace to her Creator.

SECTION IX.

OXENSTIERN.

Oxenstiern, chancellor of Sweden, was a man of great abilities, and uncorrupted integrity. On the accession of Christina to the crown of Sweden, the regency, during her minority, devolved upon him and four others: but so great was their confidence in Oxenstiern, that he was invested with the chief management of affairs; and he conducted himself with singular wisdom and uprightness. In the great schemes which he formed for the interest of his country, he was very successful; and was highly esteemed, not only by his countrymen, but by the most eminent persons in Europe.

This great statesman spent a part of his time in retirement, from which he derived the highest advantage. In his retreat, he was visited by Whitelocke, ambassador from England to Queen Christina; and in the conclusion of their discourse, he made the following very interesting observations:—"I have seen much, and enjoyed much, of this world; but I never knew how to live till now. I thank my good God, who has given me time to know him, and to know myself. All the comfort I have, and which is more than the whole world can give, is, feeling the good Spirit of God in my heart, and reading in this good book, (holding up the Bible,) that came from it."

This enlightened and experienced man then addressed the ambassador as follows: "You are now in the prime of your age and vigor, and in great favor and business: but all this will leave you, and you will one day better understand and relish what I say. You will then find, that there is more wisdom, truth, comfort, and pleasure, in retiring, and in turning your heart from the world, to the good Spirit of God, and in reading the Bible, than in all the courts, and favors of princes."

The preceding account is given by William Penn, who says he had it, more than once, from the ambassador himself. The sentiments expressed by Oxenstiern are particularly interesting, if we reflect that they came from one of the greatest and wisest men of the age, when his mind and body were sound and vigorous, and when he was best able to judge of human life, and of the happiness which is to be derived from religion.

SECTION X.

HUGO GROTIUS.

Hugo Grotius was born in Holland, in the year 1583. He possessed the most happy disposition, a profound genius, a solid judgment, and a wonderful memory. These extraordinary natural endowments had all the advantages that education could give them; and he was so happy as to find, in his own father, a pious and an able instructer, who formed his mind and his morals. Before he was fifteen, he maintained public theses in mathematics, philosophy, and law, with the highest applause: and he ventured to form plans that required very great learning, but which he executed in so finished a manner, that the republic of letters were struck with astonishment.

He strenuously engaged in the controversies respecting religious opinions, which, at that time, occupied the learned men of the Netherlands: and the part which he took in those disputes, involved him in great trouble and perplexity. He afterwards became the queen of Sweden's ambassador at Paris. This dignity, however, was not agreeable to a man of his turn of mind. His sentiments respecting it, are contained in a letter which he wrote to his father from Paris. "I am," says he, "really quite tired out with honors. A private and a quiet life alone has charms for me; and I should be very happy, if I were in a situation, in which I could employ myself upon works of piety, and works that might be useful to posterity."

He had the highest respect for religion and virtue, in whatever condition of life they were found: and how much he preferred them to all that the world could bestow, appears from the following declaration: "I would give all my learning and honor, for the plain integrity of John Urick, a poor man of great piety, who spent eight hours of his time in prayer, eight in labor, and but eight in meals, sleep, and other necessaries."

To one who admired his great industry, he returned an answer to this effect: "Ah! I have consumed much of my life, in laboriously doing nothing." And to another who enquired of him, what course of life he would advise him to take, he solemnly answered, "Be serious."

In his last sickness, which was of short duration, he appears to have been tranquil, and resigned to the will of God. He expressed his faith in Jesus Christ, and declared that his hope rested upon him. To one who mentioned to him the publican spoken of in the gospel, he humbly replied, "I am that publican;" and soon after expired.

Grotius, notwithstanding the embassies and other

public business in which he was employed, composed a great number of excellent and much admired works; the principal of which are, "A Treatise of the Rights of Peace and War;" "A Treatise on the Truth of the Christian Religion;" "Commentaries on the Holy Scriptures;" and "The History and Annals of Holland." He appears to have labored much for the benefit of his fellow-creatures; and we trust that his expressions of regret, respecting the employment of his time, proceeded from the humble state of his mind, and not from the consciousness of having neglected any important duty of life.

When great talents and learning are, from pure motives, and in true humility, consecrated to the service of truth and religion, they become acceptable offerings to our Divine Benefactor, and often eminently promote the good of mankind. But when we misapply these qualifications, suffer them to nourish pride and vanity, or attribute to them an efficacy in producing virtue and happiness that does not necessarily belong to them; they occasion an unhappy waste of our time, and lay the foundation for bitter regret in the winding up of life.

The worth and importance of those advantages are lamentably overrated, if our estimation of them is so high, and our pursuit so ardent, as to dispose us to undervalue, or disregard that most solemn injunction of our Lord: "Seek ye, first," (early, and in preference to all other things,) "the kingdom of God and his righteousness:" remembering that this is "the one thing needful."

Whilst the mind is occupied with the variety and intricacy of speculation and literary engagements, and the heart elated with the flattering distinctions which they produce, we may not sufficiently perceive the importance of this Divine injunction: but when the close of our day approaches, and the retrospect of life is made; when the ardor of pursuit has abated, and the delusions of vanity and passion are at an end; we shall form a true estimate of the worth of all sublunary attainments and possessions. We shall then, if not before, perceive that, to have our conversation in the world with simplicity and uprightness; to receive the truths of the gospel with meekness and cordiality; to be pure and humble in heart; to love our neighbors as ourselves, and God above all things; and, by these means, to secure an incorruptible and immortal inheritance; are attainments of infinitely greater moment than all the accomplishments of mind and body, and all the possessions and honors that this world can bestow.

As it is, therefore, our highest wisdom, may it also be our greatest concern, seasonably to anticipate these reflections; and so to temper and regulate all our studies, and all the engagements of this life, that they may coincide with and promote the great end of our being!

SECTION XI.

JOHN SELDEN.

John Selden, a native of Sussex, was born in the year 1584. He was profoundly learned, and skilled in the Hebrew and oriental languages, beyond any man of his time. Grotius styles him the glory of the English nation. His mind also was as great as his learning. He was hospitable, generous, and charitable; he took great delight in doing good, and in communicating his knowledge: above all, he was a sincere and eminent Christian.

The earl of Clarendon, who was the intimate friend of Selden, speaks of him thus: " Mr. Selden was a person, whom no character can flatter, or transmit in any expressions equal to his merit and virtue. He was of such stupendous learning, in all kinds and in all languages, that a man would have thought he had been entirely conversant among books, and had never spent an hour but in reading or writing: yet his humanity, courtesy, and affability, were such, that he would have been thought to have been bred in the best courts. His good nature, charity, and delight in doing good, and in communicating all he knew, exceeded that breeding. In his conversation, he was the most clear discourser, and had the best faculty in making hard things easy, and present to the understanding, of any man that hath been known."

This eminent scholar and Christian, when he was near the end of his days, declared, in a conference with Archbishop Usher, that, " though he had been very laborious in his literary enquiries, and had possessed himself of a great number of valuable books and manuscripts, upon all ancient subjects; yet he could rest the happiness of his soul on none of them, except the Holy Scriptures." He said that the following passage, in a very particular manner, affected his mind: "The Grace of God, which bringeth salvation, hath appeared unto all men; teaching us, that denying ungodliness and worldly lusts, we should live soberly, righteously, and godly, in this present world; looking for that blessed hope and glorious appearing of the great God, and our Saviour Jesus Christ; who gave himself for us, that he might redeem us from all iniquity, and purify unto himself a peculiar people, zealous of good works." This is, indeed, a most important and interesting declaration. It sets forth the universal love of God; the various duties of men, with the means of performing them; the redemption from sin through Jesus Christ; and a glorious reward to the faithful hereafter.

SECTION XII.

CARDINAL RICHELIEU.

Richelieu, an eminent cardinal and minister of state in France, was born of a noble family at the castle of Richelieu, in the year 1585. Being a man of prodigious capacity, and of a restless and insatiable ambition, he formed vast designs, which made his life a series of agitations and perplexities. He found himself frequently under the necessity of opposing the grandees of the kingdom, the royal family, the whole house of Austria, and even Louis XIII. himself.

Amidst his greatest and most arduous concerns, he did not neglect to cultivate literature, and to show himself a patron of men of letters. He manifested a particular regard for persons of the religious orders; and advanced those who were most remarkable for their abilities and virtues. He made many friends, and many enemies; but his consummate policy enabled him to triumph over all the machinations of his opponents.

When this great statesman approached the conclusion of his time, he became very serious; and acknowledged to Peter du Moulin, the celebrated

French protestant, that he had often been hurried into measures which his conscience disapproved. "That he had been urged into many irregularities, by what is called state policy; that as he could not tell how to satisfy his conscience for these deviations from rectitude, he had many temptations to disbelieve the existence of a God, a future state, and the immortality of the soul; and, by these means, to quiet the upbraidings of his mind. But in vain. So strong was the idea of God in his soul; so clear the impression of him upon the frame of the world; so unanimous the consent of mankind; and so powerful the convictions of his own conscience; that he could not avoid feeling the necessity of admitting a Supreme Being, and a future state: and he wished to live as one that must die; and to die, as one that must live for ever."

The serious state of his mind increased, as he drew near his last hour. A person who came to see him, enquired, "why he was so sad:" the cardinal replied: "The soul is a serious thing: it must either be sad here for a moment, or be sad for ever."

He died in 1642, amidst storms and perils, before he had completed his designs; leaving behind him a name, splendid indeed, but, by no means, dear and venerable.

SECTION XIII.

LORD HARRINGTON.

John, Lord Harrington, was the son of that Lord Harrington to whom King James the First committed the education of his eldest daughter, the princess Elizabeth.

He possessed excellent natural endowments, and a considerable stock of useful learning; but the great concern of his mind was, to become learned in the school of Christ, and to provide for an immortal inheritance. He manifested a principle of real charity in his heart, by his love to all who were truly religious. And so great was his compassion for his fellow-creatures in necessity, that he gave the tenth part of his yearly income to charitable uses.

At the beginning of his last sickness, he strongly apprehended that he should not recover; and therefore calmly prepared for death. He declared his faith in Christ, and his undoubted hope of salvation by him: and said, with much cheerfulness, "I fear not death, in what shape soever it may assail me."

Many excellent things were expressed by him,

during his illness. He greatly desired to depart this life, that he might be at home with his Lord and Saviour. About two hours before his death he declared, that "he still felt the comfort and joys of assured salvation, by Christ Jesus." And when the time of his departure was come, he said, " O, that joy! O, my God! when shall I be with thee?" And with the like words, expressive of a tender, heavenly frame of mind, he peacefully expired, in the twenty-third year of his age.

SECTION XIV.

SALMASIUS.

SALMASIUS, of an ancient and noble family in France, was born in the year 1596. He was a man of very extraordinary abilities, and profound erudition. He was knowing in almost every thing; in school divinity, in law, in philosophy, in criticism; and he was so consummate a linguist, that there was scarcely a language in which he had not attained a considerable proficiency. He was perfect in Greek and Latin: he understood the Hebrew, Arabic, Persic, Egyptian, Chinese, &c., and he was well acquainted with all the European languages.

His works are very numerous, and on various subjects. They gained him as much fame as strong powers and a vast erudition can procure. His name was sounded throughout Europe; and he had great offers from foreign princes, and universities. The Venetians thought his residence among them would be such an honor, that they offered him a prodigious stipend: the university of Oxford made some attempts to get him into England; and the pope invited him to settle at Rome. Cardinal Richelieu used all possible means to detain him in

France, even desiring him to make his own terms;
and Christina, queen of Sweden, showed him extraordinary marks of esteem and regard.

When this celebrated man arrived at the evening of life, and found leisure to reflect seriously on
the great end of his being, he acknowledged that
he had too much, and too earnestly, engaged in literary pursuits; and had greatly overlooked those
objects in which true and solid happiness consists.
"Oh!" said he, "I have lost an immense portion of
time; time, that most precious thing in the world!
Had I but one year more, it should be spent in
studying David's psalms, and Paul's epistles."
"Oh! sirs," said he to those about him, "mind
the world less, and God more. 'The fear of the
Lord, that is wisdom; and to depart from evil,
that is understanding.'"

CHAPTER IV.

SECTION I.

CARDINAL MAZARINE.

Julius Mazarine, a famous cardinal and prime minister of France, was born in the kingdom of Naples, in the year 1602. The greatness of his abilities was conspicuous, even in his early years; and he had the advantage of being instructed by a very able tutor. He studied the interests of the various states in Italy, and of the kingdoms of France and Spain; and became profoundly skilled in politics. It was through the interest of Cardinal Richelieu, that he was introduced into the French cabinet. That cardinal made him one of the executors of his will; and during the minority of Louis XIV. he had the charge of public affairs.

His high station and great abilities, excited the envy of the nobility of France; and this occasioned a civil war that continued several years. Mazarine was, at last, forced to retire; a price was set on his head; and even his fine library was sold. But this disgrace did not long continue. Mazarine returned to the court with more honor than he had ever enjoyed; and conducted the affairs of the kingdom with so much ability and success, that he obtained the French king's most unreserved confidence. He possessed, in an eminent degree, the power of discovering the dispositions and views of men; and of assuming a character adapted to circumstances.

He was a man of great ambition, and pursued with ardor the chase of worldly honors. But, a short time before his death, he perceived the vanity of his pursuit, and lamented the misapplication of his time and talents. He was greatly affected with the prospect of his dissolution, and the uncertainty of his future condition. This made him cry out: "Oh, my poor soul! what will become of thee? Whither wilt thou go?"

To the queen dowager of France, who came to visit him in his illness, and who had been his friend at court, he expressed himself in these terms: "Madam, your favors have undone me. Were I to live again, I would be a capuchin, rather than a courtier."

SECTION II.

BULSTRODE WHITELOCKE.

Bulstrode Whitelocke was descended from a good family in Berkshire, and born in the year 1605. He possessed strong mental powers, which were highly improved by education, study, and business. He was advanced to several stations of the greatest trust and importance, both at home and abroad, and acquitted himself in them all to the satisfaction of his employers. Whilst he was ambassador at the court of Sweden, he was particularly honored by Queen Christina.

In the latter part of his life, he withdrew from public affairs, and resided in the country till his death. In his retirement, he was visited by a friend, to whom, after making many serious observations, he expressed himself in the following manner: " I have ever thought there has been one true religion in the world; and that is the work of the Spirit of God in the hearts and souls of men. There have been, indeed, many dispensations of God, suited to his own wise ends, and adapted to the low and uncertain state of man in the world. But the old world had the Spirit of God, for it strove with them ; and the new world has had the Spirit of God, both Jew and Gentile ; and it strives with all : and they who have been led by it, have been the good people in every dispensation of God to mankind. I myself must say, that I have felt it from a child convincing me of my evil and vanity. It has often given me a true measure of this poor world, and some taste of Divine things ; and it is my grief that I did not earlier apply my soul to it. I can say, that, since my retirement from the greatness and hurries of the world, I have felt something of the work and comfort of it ; and I am persuaded that it is both ready and able to instruct, and lead, and preserve, those who will humbly and sincerely regard it. So that my religion is, the good Spirit of God in my heart; I mean, what that has wrought in me, and for me."

SECTION III.

ANNA MARIA SCHURMAN.

ANNA MARIA SCHURMAN, of a noble protestant family in Germany, was born at Cologne, in the year 1607. The powers of her mind were very great, and she employed them in the acquisition of a large stock of literature. She was skilled in many languages; and the Latin, Greek, and Hebrew were so familiar to her, that she not only wrote, but spoke them fluently, to the surprise of the most learned men. She had also a competent knowledge of the liberal arts and sciences; and was held in high reputation by several persons of the greatest learning in her time.

In the latter part of her life, the religious temper of her mind increasing, she set little value on all the honor she had acquired, by her extraordinary accomplishments; and became zealously concerned to obtain the favor of God as the richest treasure and the highest of all enjoyments. After this change of views and sentiments, she wrote an account of her life in Latin; in which she mentions some remarkable circumstances concerning herself, and several devout persons with whom she was connected.

During her last illness, she declared her full satisfaction in the religious choice she had made. After suffering much from the disorder, she expressed herself in the following manner: "I have proceeded one step further towards eternity, and if the Lord shall please to increase my pains, it will be no cause of sorrow: the will of my God is all to me; I follow him. How good is it to be in the hands of God! But it will be still better for me, when I shall enjoy more full communion with him, among the children of God, in the abodes of the blessed. I have nothing more to desire in this world."

In the last night of her life, she said to one who watched with her: "I am almost continually impressed with a sentiment of this nature: 'A Christian must suffer.' This sentiment comforts me in my pains; and supports me that I faint not. O how good it is to remain in silence and patience before God. My most beneficent Father has not dealt with me, as with his servant Job, whose friends were with him seven days in silence, and then addressed him with bitter words. But how sweet and comfortable are the impressions which I feel!"

SECTION IV.

SIR MATTHEW HALE.

Sir Matthew Hale, lord chief justice of England, was born in Gloucestershire, in the year 1609. Before he was six years old, he lost both his parents: but by the care of a judicious guardian, great attention was paid to his education. When he had completed his studies at Oxford, he quitted the university, with an intention of going into the army; but, on the persuasion of Sergeant Glanvill, he entered at Lincoln's Inn; and, with great vigor, and almost unexampled application, bent his mind to the studies of his profession.

In early life, he was fond of company, and fell into many levities and extravagances. But this propensity and conduct were corrected by a circumstance, that made a considerable impression on his mind, during the rest of his life. Being one day in company with other young men, one of the party, through excess of wine, fell down, apparently dead at their feet. Young Hale was so affected on this occasion, that he immediately retired to another room; and, shutting the door, fell on his knees, and prayed earnestly to God that his friend might be restored to life, and that he him-self might be pardoned for having given counten-ance to so much excess. At the same time, he made a solemn vow, that he would never again keep company in that manner, nor " drink a health," while he lived. His friend recovered, and Hale religiously observed his vow.

After this event, there was an entire change in his disposition : he forsook all dissipated company, and was careful to divide his time between the duties of religion, and the studies of his profession. He became remarkable for a grave and exemplary deportment, great moderation of temper, and a religious tenderness of spirit; and these virtues ap-pear to have accompanied him through the whole of his life.

The following extract from a diary which he regularly kept, shows the piety of his mind, and how solicitous he was to make the best use of his time :

MORNING.

1. To lift up the heart to God in thankfulness for renewing my life.

2. To renew my covenant with God in Christ. First, by renewed acts of faith receiving Christ, and rejoicing in the height of that relation : second-ly, by resolving to be one of his people, and doing him allegiance.

3. Adoration and prayer.

DAY EMPLOYMENT.

There must be an employment of two kinds.

1. Our ordinary calling, to serve God in it. It is a service to Christ, though ever so mean. Here observe faithfulness, diligence, cheerfulness. Not to overcharge myself with more business than I can bear.

2. Our spiritual employments. Mingle somewhat of God's immediate service in the day.

IF ALONE.

1. Beware of wandering, vain, sensual thoughts: fly from thyself rather than entertain these.

2. Let thy solitary thoughts be profitable. View the evidences of thy salvation, the state of thy soul, the coming of Christ, and thy own mortality: this will make thee humble and watchful.

COMPANY.

Do good to them. Use God's name reverently. Beware of leaving an ill impression, or ill example. Receive good from them, if they are more knowing.

EVENING.

Cast up the accounts of the day. If there was aught amiss, beg pardon; resolve to be more vigilant. If thou hast done well, bless the mercy and grace of God, which have supported thee.

Thus did this excellent man occupy himself in the service of God, at the same time that he was making great progress in the study of the sciences, and particularly in that of the law, in which he became a greater proficient than any of his contemporaries.

In the duties of his office as a judge, he conducted himself with the greatest integrity. The motives which influenced him to the faithful discharge of these duties, were founded on the only firm basis—that of religion. This will appear by an extract from one of his papers, entitled "Things to be had in continual remembrance." Among a numerous list of these, are the following:

"That, in the administration of justice, I am intrusted for God, the king, and the country: and therefore that it be done uprightly, deliberately, resolutely.

"That I rest not upon my own direction and strength; but implore and rest upon the direction and strength of God.

"That, in the execution of justice, I carefully lay aside my own passions, and give not way to them, however provoked.

"That I be not biased with compassion to the poor, or favor to the rich, in point of justice.

"That popular or court applause or dislike, have

no influence in anything I do in the distribution of justice.

"That I be not solicitous about what men think or say, so long as I keep myself exactly according to the rules of justice."

The writings of Sir Matthew Hale, on religious subjects, particularly his "Contemplations Moral and Divine," manifest a truly humble frame of mind; and contain a seriousness and fervency, well adapted to excite kindred emotions in the breast of the reader. We shall select a few of these, as testimonies which this great and good man bore to the power and efficacy of religion, as the guide, support, and comfort of our lives.

"True religion," says he, "teaches the soul a high veneration for Almighty God; a sincere and upright walking, as in the presence of the invisible, all-seeing God.

"It makes a man truly love, honor, and obey him, and therefore careful to know what his will is.

"It renders the heart highly thankful to him, as his Creator, Redeemer, and Benefactor.

"It makes a man entirely depend on him, seek him for guidance, direction, and protection, and submit to his will with patience and resignation of soul.

"It gives the law, not only to his words and actions, but to his very thoughts and purposes; so that he dares not entertain any which are unbecoming the presence of that God, by whom all our thoughts are legible.

"It crushes all pride and haughtiness, both in a man's heart and carriage, and gives him an humble state of mind before God and men.

"It regulates the passions, and brings them into due moderation.

"It gives a man a right estimate o₁ this present world, and sets his heart and hopes above it; so that he never loves it more than it deserves.

"It makes the wealth, and the glory of this world, high places, and great preferments, but of little consequence to him; so that he is neither covetous, nor ambitious, nor over-solicitous, concerning the advantages of them.

"It makes him value the love of God and the peace of his own conscience, above all the wealth and honor in the world, and to be very diligent in preserving them.

"He performs all his duties to God with sincerity and constancy: and, whilst he lives on earth, his conversation, his hope, his treasures, are in heaven; and he endeavors to walk suitably to such a hope."

His sentiments, respecting the inward direction and assistance of the Spirit of God to the soul, and his Holy Presence there, are deeply interesting.

"They who truly fear God, have a secret guidance from a higher wisdom than what is barely human, namely, the Spirit of truth and wisdom; which does really, though secretly, prevent and direct them. Any man that sincerely and truly fears Almighty God, and calls and relies upon him for his direction, has it as really as a son has the counsel and direction of his father; and though the voice is not audible, yet it is equally as real, as if a man heard a voice saying, 'This is the way, walk in it.'

"Though this secret direction of Almighty God is principally seen in matters relating to the good of the soul, yet, in the great and momentous concerns of this life, a good man, fearing God and begging his direction, will very often, if not at all times, find it. I can call my own experience to witness, that, even in the external actions, occurrences, and incidents of my whole life, I have never been disappointed of the best direction, when I have, in humility, and a sense of my own deficiency, sincerely implored it.

"God sees the most secret chambers of our hearts. All the guests that are there, even our most intimate thoughts and purposes, and much more our most retired actions, are as legible to him, as if they were graved in brass.

"Are our hearts solicited by any object—by ourselves or by the persuasions of others, or by the suggestions of Satan — to impure speculations or sinful resolutions, to proud or arrogant conceptions of ourselves, to revengeful, uncharitable, or forbidden desires, to vain and unprofitable imaginations; let us reflect that these thoughts (which even natural modesty or prudence, would shame as to express before mortal man) are all naked and manifest before the great and holy God. And dare we entertain such guests where our Creator is present? in that place which the Lord of Heaven is pleased, most justly and most mercifully to claim as his own? Consider, it is our Judge that sees us: it is the great Creator, before whom the angels of heaven veil their faces, not being able to behold his glory: and, which is more than all this to an ingenuous nature, it is he to whom we owe ourselves and all that we are, he to whom we have given up our names, and who has purchased our souls from destruction by the blood of his Son.

" Again : Is the God of heaven an eyewitness of our conduct, when either by ourselves, or by others, we are solicited to evil ?—let us take courage to resist this temptation, because our Creator sees us; because our Lord stands by, to observe, and to reward us, in our opposition. To be able to hear, in our own consciences, the approving voice of the Lord of heaven beholding us, and saying, ' Well done, good and faithful servant,' would be enough to outweigh all our obedience, though it were possible to separate it from what follows— ' Enter thou into the joy of thy Lord.' "

The following reflections on the vicissitudes of human affairs, and on the benefits to be derived from duly considering them, are highly important and instructive :—

" In the course of my life, I have been in as

many stations and places as most men. I have experienced almost continual motion ; and although,
of all earthly things, I have most desired rest, and
a fixed private station, yet the various changes that
I have seen and found, the public employments
that, without my seeking, and against my inclination, have been put upon me, and many other in-
terventions, as well private as public, have made it
literally my experience, that I have here no continuing city. When I had designed for myself a
settled mansion in one place, and had fitted it to
my convenience and repose, I have been presently
constrained, by my necessary employments, to
leave it, and repair to another : and when again I
thought to find repose there, and had suited it to
my convenience, some other necessary occurrences
have diverted me from it. And thus, my dwellings
have been like so many inns to a traveller, of
longer continuance, indeed, but of almost equal
instability.

" This unsettledness of station, though troublesome, has given me a good and practical moral ;
namely, that I must not expect my rest in this
lower world ; but must consider it as the place of
my journey and pilgrimage, and look further for
true repose and happiness. And truly, when I reflect, that it has been the wisdom of Almighty
God, to exercise, with this kind of discipline, those
worthies whom he has exhibited as patterns to the
rest of mankind, I have no reason to complain of

it, as a difficulty or an inconvenience; but to be
thankful to him for it, as an instruction and docu-
ment, to put me in remembrance of a better home,
and to incite me to make a due provision for it;
even that everlasting rest which he has provided
for them that love him: it is his gracious design,
by pouring me thus from vessel to vessel, to keep me
from fixing myself too much upon this world below.

"But the truth is, did we consider this life as
becomes us, even as wise men, we might easily
find, without the help of such discipline, that the
world below, neither was intended for, nor indeed
can be, a place of rest: but that it is only a labora-
tory to fit and prepare the souls of the children of
men, for a better and more abiding state; a school,
to exercise and train us up in habits of patience
and obedience, till we are fitted for another station; a little narrow nursery, wherein we may be
dressed and pruned, till we are fit to be transplanted into paradise.

"The shortness of our lives, and the continual
troubles, sicknesses, and calamities, that attend
them; and the instances of mortality of all ages,
sexes, and conditions of mankind, are sufficient to
convince reasonable men, who have the seriousness
and patience to consider and observe, that we have
no abiding city here. And on the other side, if we
will but give ourselves leisure to consider the great
wisdom of Almighty God, who adapts every thing
in the world to suitable ends; the excellence of the

soul and mind of man ; the great advances and improvements his nature is capable of; the admirable means which the merciful and wise God has afforded mankind, by his works of nature and providence, by his word and instructions, to qualify them for a nobler life than this world can yield ; we shall readily confess that there is another state, another city to come, which it becomes every good, and wise, and considerate man, to look after and fit himself for.

"And yet if we regard the generality of mankind with due consideration, they will appear to be a company of distempered people. The greater part of them make it their whole business to provide for rest and happiness in this world; they make the acquisition of wealth and honor, and the preferments and pleasures of life, their great, if not their only business and happiness ; and, which is yet a higher degree of phrensy, they esteem this the only wisdom ; and think that the careful provision for eternity, is the folly of a few weak, melancholy, fanciful men : whereas, it is a truth, and in due time it will evidently appear, that those men only, who are solicitous for the attaining of their everlasting rest, are the truly wise men ; and shall be acknowledged to be so, by those who now despise them. 'We fools accounted his life madness, and his end to be without honor. How is he numbered among the children of God, and his lot is among the saints !' "

This eminent and virtuous man possessed uninterrupted health, till near the sixty-sixth year of his age. At this period he was affected with an indisposition which, in a short time, greatly impaired his strength; and he found himself so unfit to discharge the duty of justice of the king's bench, that he was obliged to resign the office.

"He continued, however," says Bishop Burnet, "to retire frequently for his devotions and studies. As long as he could go himself, he went regularly to his retirement; and when his infirmities increased so that he was not able to walk to the place, he made his servants carry him thither in a chair. At last, as the winter came on, he saw with great joy his deliverance approaching: for besides his being weary of the world, and his longings for the blessedness of another state, his pains increased so much, that no patience inferior to his could have borne them without great uneasiness of mind. Yet he expressed to the last such submission to the will of God, and so equal a temper, that the powerful effects of Christianity were evident, in the support which he derived from it, under so heavy a load.

"He continued to enjoy the free use of his reason and senses to the latest moment of life. This he had often and earnestly prayed for, during his last sickness. When his voice was so sunk that he could not be heard, his friends perceived, by the almost constant lifting up of his eyes and hands, that he was still aspiring towards that blessed state, of which he was now to be speedily possessed. He had no struggles, nor seemed to be in any pangs in his last moments. He breathed out his righteous and pious soul in peace."

SECTION V.

DU RENTI.

Du Renti was a young nobleman of France, not more distinguished by his high birth, than by the excellent talents and qualifications of his mind. This accomplished youth, influenced by a strong sense of the vanity of worldly grandeur, and by an ardent desire to enjoy the comfort of a retired and religious life, believed it incumbent upon him to relinquish all his honors, and to withdraw from scenes which he feared would ensnare and corrupt his heart.

The following extracts from his views and sentiments, respecting these subjects, demonstrate, that his mind was much redeemed from the spirit and enjoyments of this world ; and that he endeavored, above all things, to obtain a holy and devout temper of heart, and to conduct himself acceptably in the Divine sight :

" When I gave up my liberty to God, I perceived to what a state of deep humiliation the soul must be brought, to render it capable of union with him. The splendor and vain enjoyments of this transitory scene, are great encumbrances to me, in my endeavors to obtain the favor of God; of which, therefore, his pleasure is that I should be stripped, in order to attain that state of humility and poorness of spirit, which will bring me into possession of real honor and solid riches.

"I find no security in any state, but in that of dying to the world, and in true self-abasement: this is to be baptized into Christ's death, and to live the life of Christian self-denial. All that can be imagined to befall us in this lower world, is comparatively of small consequence, though it were the losing of all our possessions. Had we but a little faith, and a little love, how happy should we find ourselves, in being willing to resign up every thing; and in saying, *My God, and my All!*"

How conformable are these sentiments to the Divine injunctions, "Love not the world, nor the things that are in the world."—"But be ye transformed by the renewing of your mind." It is, indeed, a holy and happy state, to be living above the world, and pressing after perfection, at the same time that we gratefully acknowledge Divine Goodness, in providing for our necessities during our passage through life. This supreme love of God, and desire to be united to him, though often cherished by retirement, is not a solitary and inactive principle. It not only purifies and exalts our minds, but it expands them towards our fellow-creatures, and leads us into acts of universal charity.

7*

SECTION VI.

PRINCESS ELIZABETH.

Princess Elizabeth, of the Rhine, was born in the year 1620. She was the eldest daughter of Frederick V., elector palatine, and king of Bohemia, by Elizabeth, daughter of James the First, king of England. This excellent princess possessed only a small territory; but she governed it with great judgment, and attention to the happiness of her subjects. She made it a rule to hear, one day in the week, all such causes as were brought before her. On these occasions, her wisdom, justice, and moderation, were very conspicuous. She frequently remitted forfeitures, in cases where the parties were poor, or in any respect worthy of favor. It was remarkable that she often introduced religious considerations, as motives to persuade the contending parties to harmony and peace. She was greatly beloved and respected by her subjects; and also by many persons of learning and virtue not resident in her dominions: for she patronized men of this character, whatever might be their country, or their religious profession.

In the year 1677, the celebrated William Penn

paid her a visit; and was treated by her with great respect. The following account of her is taken from his works :—

"The meekness and humility of the princess appeared to me extraordinary : she did not consider the quality, but the merit of the people she entertained. Did she hear of a retired man, seeking after the knowledge of a better world, she was sure to set him down in the catalogue of her charity, if he wanted it. I have casually seen, I believe, fifty tokens of her benevolence, sealed and directed to the several poor subjects of her bounty, whose distance prevented them from being personally known to her. Thus, though she kept no sumptuous table in her own court, she spread the tables of the poor in their solitary cells; breaking bread to virtuous pilgrims, according to their want and her ability.

"She was abstemious in her living; and in apparel void of all vain ornaments. I must needs say, that her mind had a noble prospect : her eye was to a better and more lasting inheritance than can be found below. This made her not overrate the honors of her station, or the learning of the schools, of which she was an excellent judge. Being once at Hamburg, a religious person, whom she went to see for her religion's sake, remarked to her, that ' it was too great an honor for him, that a visitant of her quality, who was allied to so pen great kings and princes of this world, shou taken under his roof:' to whom she humbly replied : 'If they were religious, as well as great, it would be an honor indeed; but if you knew what that greatness is, as well as I do, you would value it less.'

" After a religious meeting which we had in her chamber, she was much affected, and said : ' It is a hard thing to be faithful to what one knows. O, the way is straight! I am afraid I am not weighty enough in my spirit to walk in it !

" She once withdrew, on purpose to give her servants, who were religiously disposed, the liberty of discoursing with us, that they might the more freely put what questions of conscience they desired to be satisfied in. Sometimes she suffered both them and the poorest persons of her town, to sit by her in her own chamber, where we had two meetings. I cannot forget her last words, when I took my leave of her : ' Let me desire you to remember me, though I live at so great a distance, and you should never see me more. I thank you for this good time. Be assured, that though my condition subjects me to divers temptations, yet my soul has strong desires after the best things.'

" She lived till the age of sixty years ; and then departed at her house in Herwerden, in the year 1680, as much lamented, as she had been beloved by her people. To her real worth I do, with a religious gratitude, dedicate this memorial."

theil

In t.

SECTION VII.

WILLIAM MOMPESSON.

William Mompesson was rector of Eyam in Derbyshire, during the time of the plague that nearly depopulated the town in the year 1666, the year after that distemper prevailed in London. This benevolent man thought it his duty to continue in the place, notwithstanding the plague was making its ravages around him. He never caught the disorder; and was enabled, during the whole time of the calamity, to perform the functions of the physician, the legislator, and the priest, of his afflicted parish; assisting the sick with his medicines, his advice, and his prayers. During these pious labors, his wife was taken ill, and died.

The following letter, written by him to Sir George Saville, patron of the living of Eyam, breathes such a spirit of pure religion and resignation of mind, that we doubt not it will be acceptable to the reader :—

" Honored and Dear Sir,

" This is the saddest news that ever my pen could write! The destroying angel having taken up his quarters within my habitation, my dearest wife is gone to her eternal rest, and is invested with a crown of righteousness, having made a happy end.

"Indeed, had she loved herself as well as me, she had fled from the pit of destruction with her sweet babes, and might have prolonged her days: but she was resolved to die a martyr to my interest. My drooping spirits are much refreshed with her joys, which I think are unutterable.

"Sir, this paper is to bid you a hearty farewell for ever, and to bring you my humble thanks for all your noble favors; and I hope you will believe a dying man. I have as much love as honor for you, and I will bend my feeble knees to the God of heaven, that you, my dear lady, and your children, and their children, may be blessed with external and eternal happiness; and that the same blessing may fall upon Lady Sunderland and her relations.

"Dear sir, let your dying chaplain recommend this truth to you and your family, that no happiness or solid comfort can be found in this vale of tears, like living a pious life: and pray ever retain this rule: 'Never do anything upon which you dare not first ask the blessing of God.'

"Sir, I have made bold in my will with your name for an executor; and I hope that you will not take it ill. I have joined two others with you, who will take from you the trouble. Your favorable aspect will, I know, be a great comfort to my distressed orphans. I am not desirous that they may be great, but good; that they may be brought up in the fear and admonition of the Lord.

"Sir, I thank God I am contented to shake hands with all the world; and have many comfortable assurances that God will accept me upon the account of his Son. I find the goodness of God greater than ever I thought or imagined; and I wish, from my soul, that it were not so much abused and contemned.

"I desire, sir, that you will be pleased to make choice of an humble, pious man, to succeed me in my parsonage; and could I see your face before my departure hence, I would inform you in what manner I think he may live comfortably amongst his people; which would be some satisfaction to me before I die.

"Dear sir, I beg your prayers, and desire you to procure the prayers of all about you, that I may not be daunted by the powers of hell. With tears I beg, that when you are praying for fatherless infants, you would remember my two pretty babes.

"Pardon the rude style of this paper; and be pleased to believe that I am, dear sir,

"Your most obliged, most affectionate,

"and grateful servant,

"WILLIAM MOMPESSON.

"EYAM, Sept. 1, 1666."

SECTION VIII.

ADMIRAL PENN.

William Penn, afterwards Sir William Penn, knight and admiral of England, was born in the year 1621; and descended from an ancient family. At twenty-three years of age, he was made rear-admiral of Ireland; at thirty-one, vice-admiral of England; and at thirty-two, general in the first Dutch war. He was a member of parliament in 1655; and in 1660 was made a commissioner of the admiralty and navy, and governor of the fort and town of Kinsale.

In 1664 he was appointed chief commander under the duke of York; and was in the remarkable engagement which, in that year, happened with the Dutch fleet. He then took leave of the sea; and soon after, finding his bodily infirmities increase, he withdrew to Wanstead in Essex, where he died in 1670.

A short time before his death, looking over the busy scenes in which he had been engaged, he became solemnly impressed with the view; and filled with regret for his want of sufficient attention to the mercies he had received. The following excellent advice which, at that time, he gave to one of his sons, strongly expresses the religious state of his mind.

"Son William, I am weary of the world. I would not live over my days again, if I could command them with a wish; for the snares of life are greater than the fears of death. This troubles me, that I have offended a gracious God, who has followed me to this day. O, have a care of sin; that is the sting both of life and death. Three things I commend to you. First, let nothing in this world tempt you to wrong your conscience; I charge you, do nothing against your conscience: you will then keep peace at home, which will be a feast to you in the day of trouble.

"Secondly, whatever you design to do, plan it justly, and time it seasonably: for these give security and despatch. Lastly, be not troubled at disappointments: for if they may be recovered, do it; if they cannot, trouble is vain. If you could not have avoided them, be content: peace and profit often attend submission to Providence; and afflictions make wise. If you could have avoided them, let not your trouble exceed instruction for another time. These rules will carry you with firmness and comfort through this inconstant world."

CHAPTER V.

SECTION I.

PASCAL.

Blaise Pascal was born at Clermont in France, in the year 1623. Nature endowed him with extraordinary powers of mind, which were highly cultivated. He was an eminent philosopher, a profound reasoner, and a sublime and elegant writer. We raise his character still higher, when we say, he was a man of most exemplary piety and virtue.

The celebrated Bayle, speaking of this distinguished person, says: "A hundred volumes of religious discourses, are not of so much avail to confound the impious, as a simple account of the life of Pascal. His humility and his devotion mortify the libertines more, than if they were attacked by a dozen missionaries. They can no longer assert, that piety is confined to men of little minds, when they behold the highest degree of it in a geometrician of the first rank, the most acute metaphysician, and one of the most penetrating minds that ever existed."

From his infancy, Pascal gave proofs of a very uncommon capacity. He desired to know the reason of everything, and when sufficient reasons were not offered, he sought for better: nor would he ever yield his assent, but to such as appeared to him well-grounded. It is a comfortable reflection, that a man of this turn, with a mind so comprehensive and sagacious, entertained the most exalted sentiments of the Christian religion; and never had the least doubt of its Divine authority. This information we have from his biographer, who knew him well, and who says, "that, by the instructions and example of his father, great reverence for religion was early impressed upon his mind, and continued with him through life; and that he was always, in a high degree, opposed to the principles of infidelity."

When he was in the twenty-fourth year of his age, he declined mathematical and philosophical studies, in which he had so eminently distinguished himself, resolving to spend the remainder of his days in retirement, and to devote his time and talents wholly to the cause of piety and virtue. His work, entitled, "Thoughts upon Religion and other Subjects," has been much read and admired. He employed a great part of his time in prayer, and in reading the Holy Scriptures; and he found the greatest comfort and delight in these devout exercises. He used to say, "that the Sacred Scriptures are not so much adapted to the head, as to the heart of man; that they are intelligible only to those who have their hearts right; and that to others they are obscure and uninteresting."

In his retirement he was visited by many persons of distinction, who, on account of his great wisdom and piety, wished to consult him respecting religious subjects. His conversation abundantly answered their expectations: but he felt a fear to possess his mind, lest, on such occasions, he should speak rather to gratify his own vanity, than simply to afford information.

In the following lines, which were written by himself, and found among his papers after his decease, we see a striking picture of the mind of this good man:

"I respect poverty, because Jesus Christ respected it: I respect riches, because they furnish the means of relieving the distressed. I do not return evil to those who have done me an injury. I endeavor to be sincere and faithful to all men, but I have a peculiar tenderness towards those with whom God has caused me to be intimately connected. Whether I am alone, or in company, I consider myself as in the sight of God, who will judge my actions; and to whom I consecrate them all. These are my sentiments: and I daily bless my Redeemer, who has impressed them upon me; and who, by the operation of his grace, has taken away the concupiscence, pride, ambition, and misery, to which I was naturally subject. I owe my deliverance to his power and goodness, having nothing of myself but imbecility and corruption."

Pascal, from his youth, was much afflicted with sickness; and he often said that, from the nineteenth year of his age, he had never passed a day free from pain. He submitted to his sufferings without a murmur, and even at times rejoiced in them; believing that they came from the hand of his most merciful Father, and were designed for the purification and improvement of his soul.

During his last illness his deportment was truly edifying; and his expressions of charity and pious resignation, though deeply affecting, were highly consolatory to his friends. He said to his sister who attended him: " How has it happened that I have never done anything for the poor, though I have always had a great love for them ?" She observed to him that he had not possessed property sufficient to afford them much assistance. " Then," said he, " I ought to have given them my time and labor. In this respect I am to blame: and if my physicians speak truly, and God should permit me to recover, I am resolved that the service of the poor shall be the sole employment of my remaining days."

To some of his friends, who expressed the concern they felt on account of his great and continued afflictions, he said: "I know the dangers of health, and the advantages of sickness. When we are ill, we are exempt from many of the passions which disturb us in health; we are without ambition, without avarice; we are in continual expectation of death. We have nothing to do, but to submit humbly and peacefully."

The humility and simplicity of heart, for which he was always remarkable, seemed to increase as he approached his end. A person who frequently visited him in his last sickness, said of him: "He is a child: he is humble; he submits like a little child." One of his particular friends, who had spent an hour with him, and had been much edified by his meek and pious example, thus expressed himself to his sister: "You may, indeed, be comforted. If God should call him hence, you have abundant cause to praise that gracious Being for the favors which he has conferred upon him. I always very much admired his great qualities: but I never before observed that extraordinary simplicity which I have just now witnessed: it is wonderful in such a mind as he possesses. I most cordially wish that I were in his situation."

His last words were: "May God never forsake me!" and he died full of peace and hope.

With every deduction that can be made, for a few errors arising from peculiar circumstances, Pascal was undoubtedly one of the greatest ornaments of human nature. Few have rivalled him in talents, and few have led a life of equal innocence and piety.

SECTION II.

ROBERT BOYLE.

THE honorable ROBERT BOYLE, an eminent philosopher, and a truly good man, was the son of Richard, earl of Cork, and was born at Lismore, in Ireland, in the year 1627. At Eton school, where he was educated, he soon discovered a force of understanding, which promised great things: and a disposition to improve it to the utmost. During his education, and before he was ten years old, he was much afflicted with an ague, which considerably depressed his spirits: and to divert his attention, he was persuaded to read Amadis de Gaul, and other romantic books. But this kind of reading, he says in his memoirs, produced such restlessness in him, that he was obliged to apply himself to mathematical studies, in order to fix and settle the volatility of his fancy.

He was a man of great learning; and his stock of knowledge was immense. The celebrated Dr. Boerhaave has passed the following eulogium upon him: "Boyle was the ornament of his age and country. Which of his writings shall I commend?

All of them. To him we owe the secrets of fire, air, water, animals, vegetables, fossils : so that from his works may be deduced the whole system of natural knowledge."

He was treated with particular kindness and respect by King Charles the Second, as well as by the two great ministers, Southampton and Clarendon. By the latter he was solicited to enter into orders : for his distinguished learning, and unblemished reputation induced Lord Clarendon to think that so very respectable a personage would do great honor to the clergy.

Boyle considered the proposal with due attention. He reflected, that, in his present situation of life, whatever he wrote, with respect to religion, would have greater weight, as coming from a layman ; for he well knew that the irreligious fortified themselves against all that the clergy could offer, by supposing and saying, that it was their trade, and that they were paid for it. He considered, likewise, that, in point of fortune and character, he needed no accessions : and, indeed, his desire for these was always very limited.

But Bishop Burnet, to whom Boyle had communicated memorandums concerning his life, tells us, that what had the greatest weight, in determining his judgment, was, " the not feeling within himself any motion or tendency of mind which he could safely esteem a call from the Holy Spirit: and therefore he did not venture to take holy orders, lest he should be found to have lied unto it."

Bishop Burnet, who was Boyle's particular friend, and who, during an intimacy of twenty-nine years, had spent many happy hours in conversation with him, gives a full account of his genuine piety and virtue, and of his zeal for the Christian religion. "This zeal," he says, " was unmixed with narrow notions, or a bigoted heat in favor of a particular sect: it was that spirit which is the ornament of a true Christian." Burnet mentions, as a proof of this, his noble foundation for lectures in defence of the gospel, against infidels of all sorts; the effects of which have been very conspicuous in the many volumes of excellent discourses which have been published in consequence of that laudable and pious design.

He was at the charge of the translation and impression of the New Testament, into the Malayan tongue: and he had it dispersed in the East Indies. He gave a great reward to the person who translated into Arabic, Grotius's incomparable book, on the truth of the Christian religion; and had a whole edition printed at his own expense, which he took care to have spread in all the countries where that language was understood. By munificent donations, and by his patronage, he also very materially promoted the plans of other persons, for propagating the Christian religion, in remote parts of the world. In other respects, his charities were so extensive, that they amounted to more than a thousand pounds sterling every year.

The great object of his philosophical pursuits, was, to promote the cause of religion, and to discountenance atheism and infidelity. His intimate friend, Bishop Burnet, makes the following observations on this point: "It appeared to those who conversed with him on his inquiries into nature, that his main design, (on which, as he had his own eye constantly fixed, so he took care to put others often in mind of it,) was to raise in himself and others, more exalted sentiments of the greatness and glory, the wisdom and goodness of God. This design was so deeply impressed on his mind, that he concludes the article of his will which relates to the Royal Society, in these words: 'I wish them a happy success in their attempts to discover the true nature of the works of God: and I pray that they, and all other searchers into physical truths, may cordially refer their attainments, to the glory of the great Author of nature, and to the comfort of mankind.'"

On another occasion, the same person speaks of him thus: "He had the most profound veneration for the great God of heaven and earth, that I ever observed in any man. The very name of God was never mentioned by him, without a pause and observable stop in his discourse." So brightly did the example of this great and good man shine, through his whole course, that Bishop Burnet, on reviewing it, in a moment of pious exultation, thus expressed himself: " I might challenge the whole tribe of libertines, to come and view the usefulness, as well as the excellence of the Christian religion, in a life that was entirely dedicated to it."

SECTION III.

JOHN LOCKE.

JOHN LOCKE, a very celebrated philosopher, and one of the greatest men that England ever produced, was born in the year 1632. He was well educated; and applying himself with vigor to his studies, his mind became enlarged, and stored with much useful knowledge. He went abroad as secretary to the English ambassador at several of the German courts; and afterwards had the offer of being made envoy at the court of the emperor, or of any other that he chose: but he declined the proposal, on account of the infirm state of his health.

He was a commissioner of trade and plantations, in which station he very honorably distinguished himself. Notwithstanding his public employments, he found leisure to write much for the benefit of mankind. His "Essay on the Human Understanding," his "Discourses on Government," and his "Letters on Toleration," are justly held in high estimation.

This enlightened man and profound reasoner was most firmly attached to the Christian religion. His zeal to promote it appeared, first, in his middle age, by publishing a discourse to demonstrate the reasonableness of believing Jesus to be the promised Messiah ; and, afterwards, in the latter part of his life, by a very judicious Commentary on several of the Epistles of the Apostle Paul.

The sacred Scriptures are everywhere mentioned by him with the greatest reverence ; and he exhorts Christians, " to betake themselves in earnest to the study of the way to salvation, in those holy writings, wherein God has revealed it from heaven, and proposed it to the world ; seeking our religion where we are sure it is in truth to be found, comparing spiritual things with spiritual."

In a letter, written the year before his death, to a person who asked this question, " What is the shortest and surest way for a young man to attain the true knowledge of the Christian religion ?" he says : " Let him study the Holy Scriptures, especially the New Testament. Therein are contained the words of eternal life. It has God for its author ; salvation for its end ; and truth without any mixture of error, for its matter."

This advice was conformable to his own practice. " For fourteen or fifteen years, he applied himself, in an especial manner, to the study of the Scriptures, and employed the last years of his life hardly in anything else. He was never weary of admiring the great views of that sacred book, and the just relation of all its parts : he every day made discoveries in it, that gave him fresh cause of admiration."

The consolation which he derived from Divine revelation, is forcibly expressed in these words : " I gratefully receive and rejoice in the light of revelation, which has set me at rest in many things, the manner whereof my poor reason can by no means make out to me."

After he had diligently employed a great part of his life in a variety of occupations, he chose a pleasing retirement for the remainder of his days. This leisure appears to have been productive of solid improvement, by enabling him to look calmly over the scenes of past life ; to form a proper estimate of its enjoyments ; and to dedicate himself more fully to the cause of piety and virtue.

The summer before his death, he began to be very sensible of his approaching dissolution. He often spoke of it, and always with great composure. A short time before his decease, he declared to a friend, that " he was in the sentiments of perfect charity towards all men ; and of a sincere union with the church of Christ, under whatever name distinguished."

The day before his death, Lady Masham being alone with him, and sitting by his bedside, he exhorted her to regard this world only as a state of preparation for a better ; adding, that " he had lived long enough, and thanked God for having passed his days so comfortably ; but that this life appeared to him mere vanity." His meaning, in this last expression, doubtless was, that the duration and enjoyment of this life are as nothing, compared with the endless ages, and the supreme felicity, of the life which is to come.

The same day, he particularly advised all about him to read the Scriptures; and desired to be remembered by them at evening prayers. Being told that, if he chose it, the whole family should be with him in his chamber, he said, he should be very glad to have it so, if it would not give too much trouble: and an occasion offering to speak of the goodness of God, he especially exalted the care which God showed to man in justifying him by faith in Jesus Christ; and, in particular, returned God thanks, for having blessed him with the knowledge of the Divine Saviour.

About two months before his death, he wrote a letter to his friend, Anthony Collins, and left this direction upon it: "To be delivered to him after my decease." It concludes with the following remarkable words:—

" May you live long and happy, in the enjoyment of health, freedom, content, and all those blessings which Providence has bestowed on you, and to which your virtue entitles you. You loved me living, and will preserve my memory when I am dead. All the use to be made of it is, that this life is a scene of vanity, which soon passes away, and affords no solid satisfaction, but in the consciousness of doing well, and in the hopes of another life. This is what I can say upon experience; and what you will find to be true, when you come to make up the account. Adieu."

The following extract from a letter written by Lady Masham, deserves a place among the testimonies respecting this distinguished and excellent man:

"You will not, perhaps, dislike to know, that the last scene of Mr. Locke's life, was not less admirable than anything else concerning him. All the faculties of his mind were perfect to the last. His weakness, of which only he died, made such gradual and visible advances, that few people, I think, do so sensibly see death approach them, as he did. During all this time, no one could observe the least alteration in his humor: always cheerful, conversable, civil; to the last day thoughtful of all the concerns of his friends, and omitting no fit occasion of giving Christian advice to all about him. In short, his death was, like his life, truly pious; yet natural, easy, and unaffected. Time, I think, can never produce a more eminent example of reason and religion than he was, both living and dying."

8*

SECTION IV.

JOHN JANEWAY.

John Janeway was born in Hertfordshire, in the year 1633. He was remarkable for his piety and love of mankind, for an exemplary conduct through life, and a happy, triumphant death.

Before he was thirteen years of age, he had made a considerable proficiency in the mathematics, in the science of astronomy, and in other branches of useful literature. At the age of seventeen, he was chosen to King's College in Cambridge; and when he was about eighteen, it pleased Divine Goodness to open his understanding, and discover to him, that the knowledge of his Creator, and a consciousness of an interest in his love, through Jesus Christ, was infinitely superior to every attainment and possession of this world. At this time, he became sensible that astronomy surveys but a molehill, in comparison of the great objects which the religion of Jesus contemplates.

The complacency and delight which he found in a religious life, were discernible in his very countenance. Though he had a just sense of the value of learning and knowledge, yet he now " counted everything but as dross and dung, in comparison of the knowledge of Christ, and him crucified." From this period of his life to the conclusion of it, he continued to rise above the world, and to labor for purity of heart, and acceptance in the Divine sight.

As his own comforts came from the source of all consolation, so he was desirous of leading others to partake of that fountain, and to depend upon it for support. "We poor foolish creatures," said he, on a particular occasion, "scarcely know what is good for ourselves: but it is no small encouragement to the people of God, that wisdom itself is their guard; and that one who loves them better than they love themselves, cares for them."

When he fell into a decline, and had but little prospect of life, he was far from being alarmed with the view of his dissolution. "I am ashamed," he said, "to desire and pray for life. Is there anything here, more desirable than the enjoyment of Jesus Christ? Can I desire anything below comparable to that blessed vision? O that crown! that rest which remains for the people of God! and, blessed be God, I can say, I know it is mine."

It was his custom to set apart an hour every day, for secret retirement and solemn meditation. On one of these occasions, a friend of his, unknown to him, placed himself in a situation, where he observed all that passed; and his remarks on the scene before him, are worthy of insertion. "What a spectacle did I behold! Surely, a man walking with God, conversing intimately with him, and maintaining a holy freedom with the great Jehovah. Methought I saw a spiritual merchant in a heavenly exchange, pursuing a rich trade for the treasures of the other world. O what an animating sight it was! methinks I see him still. How lovely was his countenance! His looks, and smiles, and every motion, spoke him to be upon the confines of glory."

He was full of love and compassion to the souls of men; and often greatly lamented the barrenness of Christians, in their converse with each other.

" O," said he, on a particular occasion, "to spend an hour or two together, and to hear scarcely a word that speaks people's hearts in love with holiness! Where is our love to God, and our fellow-creatures, all this while? Where is our sense of the preciousness of time? of the greatness of our account? Should we talk thus, if we believed we should hear of it again at the day of judgment? Does not this speak aloud that our hearts are devoid of grace; and that we have little sense of spiritual and eternal concerns?"

To a friend who visited him, and who spoke of the excellence of Christ, and of the glory of the invisible world, he replied: "Ah! I feel something of it. My heart is as full as it can hold in this lower state."

Though he was, generally, as he approached his end, in a triumphant frame of spirit, yet he experienced, at times, some variations: and in these seasons, he used to say: "Hold out, faith and patience, yet a little while, and your trial will be over."

Near the close of life, most of his work was praise. Admiring the boundless love of God to him, he said: "O, why this love to me, Lord? why to me? Praise is now my work, and I shall be engaged in that sweet employment for ever. O, help me to praise him! I have nothing else to do. I have done with prayer; I have almost done with conversing with mortals. I shall soon behold Christ himself, who died for me, and loved me, and washed me in his blood. I shall shortly be in eternity, singing the song of Moses, and the song of the Lamb. I shall presently stand upon Mount Sion, with an innumerable company of angels, and the spirits of the just made perfect. I shall hear the voice of multitudes, and be one amongst them who say, 'Hallelujah! salvation, glory, and honor, and power, unto the Lord our God!'"

Thus did this favored and happy spirit take his leave of the world, and rise triumphant to the regions of bliss and immortality. He died in the twenty-fifth year of his age.

SECTION V.

EARL OF MARLBOROUGH.

JAMES, EARL OF MARLBOROUGH, was killed in a battle at sea, on the coast of Holland, in the year 1665. Not long before his death, he had a presentiment of it; and wrote to his friend, Sir Hugh Pollard, a letter, of which the following is an extract:—

"I believe the goodness of your nature, and the friendship you have always borne me, will receive with kindness the last office of your friend. I am in health enough of body, and, through the mercy of God in Jesus Christ, well disposed in mind. This I premise, that you may be satisfied that what I write proceeds not from any fantastic terror of mind, but from a sober resolution of what concerns myself, and an earnest desire to do you more good after my death, than my example, (God of his mercy pardon the badness of it!) in my lifetime, may do you harm.

"I will not speak aught of the vanity of this world: your own age and experience will save that labor. But there is a certain thing called Religion, dressed fantastically, and to purposes bad enough,

which yet, by such evil dealing, loseth not its
being. The great, good God hath not left it without a witness, more or less, sooner or later, in
every man's bosom, to direct us in the pursuit of
it ; and for avoiding those inextricable disquisitions
and entanglements, our own frail reason would per-
plex us with, God, in his infinite mercy, hath given
us his holy word, in which, as there are many
things hard to be understood, so there is enough
plain and easy, to quiet our minds, and direct us
concerning our future being. I confess to God
and you, I have been a great neglecter, and, I fear,
despiser of it : God, of his infinite mercy, pardon
me the dreadful fault ! But when I retired myself
from the noise and deceitful vanity of the world, I
found no true comfort in any other resolution than
what I had from thence. I commend, from the
bottom of my heart, the same to your, I hope,
happy use.

"Dear Hugh, let us be more generous, than to
believe we die as the beasts that perish ; but with
a Christian, manly, brave resolution, look to what
is eternal. The only great and holy God, Father,
Son, and Holy Ghost, direct you to a happy end of
your life, and send us a joyful resurrection. So
prays your true friend,

MARLBOROUGH."

This letter marks the writer's strong sense of
the importance of the sacred writings ; and his

deep regret for having, at any period, treated them with indifference. When our pursuits in life, our companions, or our taste for a particular species of reading, occasion us to contemn or neglect the Holy Scriptures, and the simplicity of the Gospel, it is a sad proof that the mind has begun to be perverted, and that the way is prepared for great depravity of heart. Whatever, therefore, tends to lessen our esteem for those venerable and highly interesting communications of the Divine Will; or disinclines us to the perusal and study of them; should be regarded with early apprehension, and avoided with the utmost solicitude.

"The Scriptures," says Bishop Horne, "are wonderful, with respect to the matter which they contain, the manner in which they are written, and the effects which they produce. They contain the sublimest truths, many of which are veiled under external ceremonies and figurative descriptions. When they are properly opened and enforced, they terrify and humble, they convert and transform, they console and strengthen. Who but must delight to study, and to observe these testimonies of the will and the wisdom, the love and the power of God most high! While we have these holy writings, let us not waste our time, misemploy our thoughts, and prostitute our admiration, by doating on human follies, and wondering at human trifles."

CHAPTER VI

SECTION I.

LADY RACHEL RUSSEL.

Lady Rachel Russel, daughter of the earl of Southampton, was born about the year 1636. She appears to have possessed a truly noble mind, a solid understanding, an amiable and a benevolent temper. Her pious resignation, and religious deportment, under the pressure of very deep distress, afford a highly instructive example, and an eminent instance of the Power of Religion to sustain the mind, in the greatest storms and dangers, when the waves of affliction threaten to overwhelm it.

It is well known, that the husband of this lady, William, Lord Russel, was beheaded in the reign of Charles the Second; that he was a man of great merit; and that he sustained the execution of his severe sentence, with Christian and invincible fortitude. During the period of her illustrious husband's troubles, she conducted herself with a mixture of the most tender affection, and the most surprising magnanimity. She appeared in court at his trial; and when the attorney-general told him, "IIe might employ the hand of one of his servants in waiting, to take notes of the evidence for his use," Lord Russel answered, "that he asked none, but that of the lady who sat by him." The spectators, at these words, turned their eyes, and beheld the daughter of the virtuous Southampton rising up to assist her lord in this his utmost distress: a thrill of anguish ran through the assembly. After his condemnation she threw herself at the king's feet; and pleaded, but alas! in vain, the merits and loyalty of her father, in order to save her husband.

When the time of separation came, her conduct appears to be worthy of the highest admiration: for without a sigh or tear, she took her last farewell of her husband, though it might have been expected, as they were so happy in each other, and no wife could possibly surpass her in affection, that the torrent of her distress would have overflowed its banks, and been too mighty for restraint.

Lord Russel parted from his lady with a composed silence: and observing how greatly she was supported, said after she was gone: "The bitterness of death is now past:" for he loved and esteemed her beyond expression. IIe declared, that "she had been a great blessing to him; and observed, that he should have been miserable, if she had not possessed so great magnanimity of spirit joined to her tenderness, as never to have desired him to do a base thing to save his life." He said, "there was a signal providence of God, in giving him such a wife, in whom were united noble birth and fortune, great understanding, great religion, and great kindness to himself; but that her behavior in his extremity, exceeded all."

After the death of her lord upon the scaffold, this excellent woman, encompassed with the darkest clouds of affliction, seemed to be absorbed in a religious concern, to behave properly under the afflicting hand of God ; and to fulfill the duties now devolved upon herself alone, in the care, education, disposal, and happiness of her children ; those living remains of her lord, which had been so dear to him, and which were, for his sake, as well as their own, so dear to herself.

The following short extracts from a few of her letters, evince the humble and pious frame of her mind ; the great benefits she derived from her afflictions ; and the comfortable hope she entertained of her future rest and felicity :—

"You, my friend, who knew us both, and how we lived, must allow I have just cause to bewail my loss. I know it is common with others to lose a friend : but few can glory in the happiness of having lived with such a one ; and few, consequently, can lament the like loss. Who but must shrink at such a blow, till, by the mighty aid of the Holy Spirit, they let the gift of God, which he has put into their hearts, interpose? O! if I did steadfastly believe, I could not be dejected: for I will not injure myself to say, I offer my mind any inferior consolation to supply this loss. No; I most willingly forsake this world, this vexatious, troublesome world; in which I have no other business, than to rid my soul from sin, and secure my eternal interests; to bear with patience and courage my eminent misfortunes, and ever hereafter to be above the smiles and frowns of it: and, having finished the remnant of the work appointed me on earth, joyfully to wait for the heavenly perfection in God's good time; when, by his infinite mercy, I may be counted worthy to enter into the same place of rest and repose, where he is gone for whom I grieve."

"The future part of my life will not, I expect, pass as perhaps I would choose. Sense has long enough been satisfied; indeed so long, that I know not how to live by faith; yet the pleasant stream, that fed it near fourteen years together, being gone, I have no sort of refreshment, but when I can repair to that living Fountain, whence all flows; while I look not at the things which are seen, but at those which are not seen, expecting that day which will settle and compose all my tumultuous thoughts, in perpetual peace and quiet."

"The consideration of the other world is not only very great, but in my small judgment, the only support under the greatest of afflictions that can befall us here. The enlivening heat of those glories is sufficient to animate and refresh us, in our dark passage through this world: and notwithstanding I am below the meanest of God's servants, and have not, in the least degree, lived answerably to those opportunities I have had; yet my Mediator is my judge, and he will not despise weak beginnings, though there be more smoke than flame. He will help us in believing; and, though he suffer us to be cast down, will not cast us off, if we commit our cause to him.

"I strive to reflect how large my portion of good things has been: and though they are passed away, no more to return, yet I have a pleasant work to do, to dress up my soul for my desired change, and to fit it for the converse of angels, and the spirits of just men made perfect; among whom, my hope is, my loved lord is one; and my often-repeated prayer to God is, that if I have a reasonable ground for that hope, it may give refreshment to my poor soul."

"From the enticing delights of the world, I can, after this event, be better weaned. I was too rich in possessions, while I possessed him. All relish now is gone. I bless God for it; and pray that I may more and more turn the stream of my affections upwards, and set my heart upon the ever-satisfying perfections of God; not starting at his darkest providences, but remembering continually, that either his glory, justice, or power, is advanced by every one of them, and that mercy is over all his works; as we shall one day, with ravishing delight, behold. In the meantime, I endeavor to suppress all wild imaginations, which a melancholy mind is apt to let in; and to say, with the man in the Gospel, ' I believe; help thou my unbelief.' "

" It is the grace of God which disposes me to ask for, and thirst after, such comforts as the world cannot give. What comforts it can give, I am most sure I have felt, and experienced to be uncertain and perishing. Such I will never more, the grace of God assisting, look after; and yet I expect a joyful day, after some mournful ones; and though I walk sadly through the valley of death, I will fear no evil, humbling myself under the mighty hand of God, who will save in the day of trouble. He knows my sorrows, and the weakness of my person : I commit myself and mine to him. The saddest state to a good soul, will one day end in rest. This is my best comfort, and a greater we cannot have; yet the degree is raised, when we consider that we shall not only rest, but live in regions of unspeakable bliss. This should lead us sweetly through the dark passage of the world; and suffer us to start at nothing we either meet with, or our fears suggest may happen to us."

To Lady Essex she wrote as follows:—"I be-seech God one day to speak peace to our afflicted minds, and not to suffer us to be disappointed of our great hope. But we must wait for our day of consolation, till this world passes away: an unkind and trustless world this has been to us. Why it has been such, God knows best. All his dispensations serve the end of his providence. They are ever beautiful, and must be good, and good to every one of us; and even these dismal ones are so to us, if we can bear evidence to our own souls, that we are better for our afflictions; which is often the case with those who suffer wrongfully. We may reasonably believe our friends have found that rest we yet but hope for; and what better comfort can you or I desire, in this valley of the shadow of death we are walking through? The rougher our path is, the more delightful and ravishing will be the great change."

She survived Lord Russel above forty years: and continued his widow to the end of her life. She died in the year 1723, in the eighty-seventh year of her age. Her continued hope and trust in HIM, who had been the staff of her life, and her support in affliction, is evidenced by the following declaration, made not long before the end of her days: " God has not denied me the support of his Holy Spirit, in this my long day of calamity, but he has enabled me, in some measure, to rejoice in him as my portion for ever. He has provided a remedy for all our griefs, by his sure promises of another life; where there is no death, nor any pain nor trouble, but fulness of joy, in the presence of him who made us, and who will love us for ever."

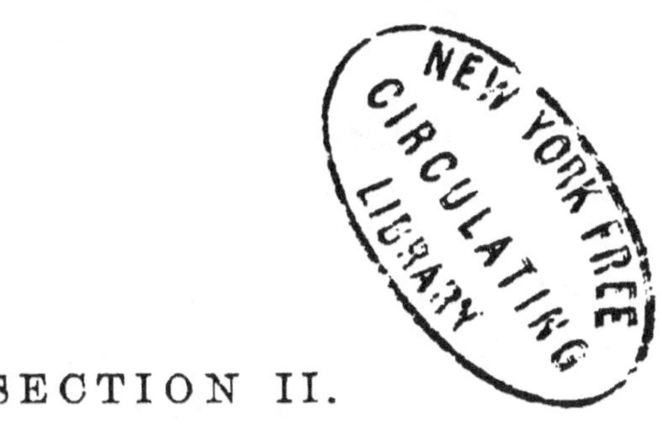

SECTION II.

JANE RATCLIFFE.

JANE RATCLIFFE was born about the year 1600. Her extraordinary faith and piety render her a suitable subject for these memoirs.

In early life, she indulged herself in many of the follies and vanities of her time; but being awakened to a sense of their fatal tendency, she renounced them; and placed her affections on objects which alone can confer solid and durable enjoyment. We shall pass over the intermediate parts of her circumspect life, and come to the closing scene of it, when she appeared to be much raised above the love of life, and the fears of death. The following is an extract from her own expressions, on that solemn occasion. At the same time that they manifest her desire to be released from the sorrows and dangers of mortality, there can be no doubt that it was limited by a humble submission, and pious resignation, to the will of Heaven:

"I desire to die," said she, "because I want, while I live here, the glorious presence of God, which I love and long for; and the sweet fellowship of angels and saints, who would be as glad to see me with them, as I should be to see them about me; and who would entertain me with unwearied delight.

"I desire to die—because, while I live, I shall want the perfection of my nature, and be as an estranged and banished child from my father's house.

"I desire to die—because I would not live to offend so good a God, and grieve his Holy Spirit. For his loving-kindness is better than life, and he is abundant in mercy to me; and the fear of displeasing him often lies as a heavy load upon my heart.

"I desire to die—because this world is generally infected with the plague of sin, and I myself am tainted with the same disease: so that, while I live here, I shall be in danger of being infected, or of infecting others. And if this world hates me, because I endeavor to follow goodness, how would it rejoice, if my foot should slip! How woful would my life be to me, if I should give occasion to the world to triumph and blaspheme! There are in my nature so many defects, errors, and transgressions, that I may say with David, 'Innumerable evils have compassed me about: my iniquities have taken hold on me, so that I am not able to look up.' I therefore desire heaven for holiness, and to the end I may sin no more.

"I desire to die—because nothing in this world can give me solid and durable contentment.

"With regard to my children, I am not troubled;

for that God who has given them life and breath,
and all they have, while I am living, can provide
for them when I am dead. My God will be their
God, if they be his: and if they be not, what comfort would it be for me to live to behold it! Life
would be bitter to me, if I should see them dishonor God, whom I so greatly love.

"I fear not death—because it is but the separation of the soul from the body: and that is but the
shadow of the body of death. Whereas, the separation of the soul from God by sin, and of soul and
body for sin, is death indeed.

"I fear not death—because it is an enemy that
has been often vanquished; and because I am
armed for it; and the weapons of my warfare are
mighty through God, and I am assured of victory.

"I do not fear death for the pain of it; for I am
persuaded I have endured as great pain in life, as I
shall find in death; and death will cure me of all
sorts of pain. Besides, Christ died a terrible death,
to the end any kind of death might be blessed to
me. And that God who has greatly loved me in
life, will not neglect me in death; but will, by his
Spirit, succor and strengthen me all the time of the
combat."

For her comfort in her last hours, she put into
the following form, some memoirs of the principal
mercies and blessings she had received from God:

"How shall I praise God for my conversion? for
his word, both in respect of my affection to it, and

the wonderful comforts I have had from it? for
hearing my prayers? for godly sorrow? for fellowship with the godly? for joy in the Holy Spirit?
for the desire of death? for contempt of the world?
for private helps and comforts? for giving me some
strength against my sins? for preserving me from
gross evils, both before and after my calling?"

In her last sickness, which was of long continuance, she was deeply sensible of the dangers and
miseries that attend our progress through life; and
often implored God to remove her into a better
world, saying, in the words of David: "Make haste
to help me, O Lord, my salvation! Be pleased, O
Lord, to deliver me! O Lord, make haste to help
me!" And she was relieved in the tenderest manner: for her spirit departed from the body, when it
was thought she had only fallen asleep. She died
in the year 1638.

SECTION III.

SIR ISAAC NEWTON.

SIR ISAAC NEWTON, a most celebrated English philosopher and mathematician, and one of the greatest geniuses that ever appeared in the world, was descended from an ancient family in Lincolnshire, where he was born, in the year 1642. His powers of mind were wonderfully comprehensive and penetrating. Fontenelle says of him, that "in learning mathematics, he did not study Euclid, who seemed to him too plain and simple, and unworthy of taking up his time. He understood him almost before he read him: a cast of his eye on the contents of the theorems of that great mathematician, seemed to be sufficient to make him master of them." Several of his works mark a profundity of thought and reflection, that has astonished the most learned men.

He was highly esteemed by the university of Cambridge; and was twice chosen to represent that place in Parliament. He was also greatly favored by Queen Anne, and by George the First. The princess of Wales, afterwards queen-consort of England, who had a turn for philosophical inquiries, used frequently to propose questions to him. This princess had a great regard for him; and often declared that she thought herself happy to live at the same time as he did, and to have the pleasure and advantage of his conversation.

This eminent philosopher was remarkable for being of a very meek disposition, and a great lover of peace. He would rather have chosen to remain in obscurity, than to have the serenity of his days disturbed by those storms and disputes, which genius and learning often draw upon those who are eminent for them. We find him reflecting on the controversy respecting his optic lectures, (in which he had been almost unavoidably engaged,) in the following terms: "I blamed my own imprudence, for parting with so real a blessing as my quiet, to run after a shadow."

The amiable quality of modesty stands very conspicuous in the character of this great man's mind and manners. He never spoke, either of himself or others, in such a manner as to give the most malicious censurers the least occasion even to suspect him of vanity. He was candid and affable, and he did not assume any airs of superiority over those with whom he associated. He never thought either his merit or his reputation, sufficient to excuse him from any of the common offices of social life.

Though he was firmly attached to the Church of England, he was averse to the persecution of the

Non-conformists. He judged of men by their conduct: and the true schismatics, in his opinion, were
the vicious and the wicked. This liberality of sentiment did not spring from the want of religion;
for he was thoroughly persuaded of the truth of
Revelation: and amidst the great variety of books,
which he had constantly before him, that which he
loved the best, and studied with the greatest application, was the Bible. He was, indeed, a truly pious
man: and his discoveries concerning the frame and
system of the universe, were applied by him to
demonstrate the being of a God, and to illustrate
his power and wisdom. He also wrote an excellent
discourse, to prove that the remarkable prophecy
of Daniel's weeks, was an express prediction of the
coming of the Messiah, and that it was fulfilled in
Jesus Christ.

The testimony of the pious and learned Dr. Doddridge to the most interesting part of this great
man's character, cannot be omitted on the present
occasion. "According to the best information,"
says he, "whether public or private, I could ever
obtain, his firm faith in the Divine Revelation, discovered itself in the most genuine fruits of substan-
tial virtue and piety; and consequently gives us the
justest reason to conclude, that he is now rejoicing
in the happy effects of it, infinitely more than all
the applause which his philosophical works have
procured him, though they have commanded a
fame lasting as the world."

The disorder of which he died, was, at times, attended with paroxysms so severe as to occasion large drops of sweat to run down his face. In these trying circumstances, he was never heard to utter the least complaint, nor to express the least impatience. He died in the eighty-fifth year of his age. In his principles, and conduct through life, he has left a strong and comfortable evidence, that the highest intellectual powers harmonize with religion and virtue; and that there is nothing in Christianity but what will abide the scrutiny of the soundest and most enlarged understanding.

How great and satisfactory a confirmation is it to the sincere, humble Christian, and what an insurmountable barrier does it present to the infidel, to perceive, in the list of Christian believers, the exalted and venerable names of Bacon, Boyle, Locke, Newton, Addison, Lyttleton, and Jones! men who must be acknowledged to be ornaments of human nature, when we consider the wide compass of their abilities, the great extent of their learning and knowledge, and their piety, their zeal for truth, and their beneficence. These eminent characters firmly adhered to the belief of Christianity, after the most diligent and exact researches into the life of its Founder, the authenticity of its records, the completion of its prophecies, the sublimity of its doctrines, the purity of its precepts, and the arguments of its adversaries.

SECTION IV.

BISHOP BURNET

Gilbert Burnet, bishop of Salisbury, was born at Edinburgh, in the year 1643. He was carefully educated by his father; and having a strong constitution and a prodigious memory, he applied himself closely to study, and acquired a great portion of learning and knowledge, which he seemed to have ready for all occasions. He travelled through France, Italy, and Holland; where he formed connections with many of the greatest persons of his time, by whom he was much respected for his talents and virtues. At Amsterdam, he became acquainted with the leading men of the different persuasions tolerated in the Netherlands, Calvinists, Arminians, Lutherans, Anabaptists, Brownists, Papists, and Unitarians; among each of which, he used frequently to declare, he met with men of such unfeigned piety and virtue, that he became strongly fixed in a principle of universal charity, and an invincible abhorrence of all severities on account of religious opinions.

He was instrumental in promoting the Revolution; and lived in great favor with William and

Mary, and Queen Anne. He distinguished himself in the House of Lords, by declaring for moderate measures, with regard to the clergy who scrupled to take the oaths; and for a toleration of the Protestant dissenters. He composed many works, which evince his desire to promote the cause of piety and virtue. "The History of his own Time," and "The History of the Reformation," have been much read; and for the latter he received the thanks of both houses of Parliament. His account of Lord Rochester, is an elegant and interesting performance; and a striking display of the truth and excellence of the Christian religion.

The last five or six years of his life he became more abstracted from the world; and he seems to have derived great advantage from the reflections which this leisure produced. The following sentiments, solemnly expressed by him towards the conclusion of his days, are so illustrative of the nature and power of true religion, and of its influence upon his own mind, that they claim a place in these memorials :

"I shall conclude with recommending to all sorts of men, in the most solemn and serious manner, the study and practice of religion, as that which is the most important of all things, and which is both the light of the world, and the salt of the earth.

"Nothing so opens our faculties and composes and directs the whole man, as an inward sense of God; of his authority over us; of the laws he has

set us; of his eye ever upon us; of his hearing
our prayers; assisting our endeavors; watching over
our concerns; of his being to judge, and reward
or punish us in another state according to what we
have done in this. Nothing will give us such a
detestation of sin, and such a sense of the goodness of God, and of our obligations to holiness, as
a right understanding and firm belief of the Christian religion.

"By living according to the rules of religion, a
man becomes the wisest, the best, and the happiest creature that he is capable of being. Honest
industry, the employing of time well, a constant
sobriety, an undefiled purity and chastity, with continued serenity, are the best preservatives too of
life and health: so that take a man as an individual, religion is his guard, his perfection, his beauty, and his glory. This will make him a light in
the world, shining brightly, and enlightening many
round about him.

"Thus, religion, if truly received and sincerely
adhered to, would prove the greatest of all blessings to a nation. But, by religion, I understand
something more than receiving particular doctrines, though ever so true, or professing them, and
engaging to support them, even with zeal and
eagerness. What signify the best doctrines, if
men do not live suitably to them; if they have not
a due influence upon their thoughts and their lives?
Men of bad lives, with sound opinions, are self-

condemned, and lie under a highly-aggravated guilt.

"By religion, I do not mean an outward compliance with forms and customs, in going to church, to prayers, to sermons, and to sacraments, with an external show of devotion; or, which is more, with some inward forced good thoughts, in which many satisfy themselves, while these have no visible effect on their lives; nor any inward force to control and rectify their appetites, passions and secret designs. These customary performances, how good and useful soever when understood and rightly directed, are of little value when men rest on them, and think, because they do them, they have acquitted themselves of their duty, though they still continue proud, covetous, full of deceit, envy, and malice. Even secret prayers, the most effectual means, are designed for a higher end; which is, to possess our minds with such a constant and present sense of Divine truths, as may make these live in us, and govern us, and draw down such assistance, as to exalt and sanctify our natures.

"So that, by religion, I mean such a sense of Divine truth as enters into a man, and becomes the spring of a new nature within him; reforming his thoughts and designs; purifying his heart; sanctifying and governing his whole deportment, his words as well as his actions; convincing him that it is not enough not to be scandalously vicious, or to be innocent in his conversation; but that he must be entirely, uniformly, and constantly, pure and virtuous, animated with zeal to be still better and better, more eminently good and exemplary.

" This is true religion, which is the perfection of human nature, and the joy and delight of every one that feels it active and strong within him. It is true, this is not arrived at all at once; and it will have an unhappy alloy, hanging long even about a good man : but, as those ill mixtures are the perpetual grief of his soul, so that it is his chief care to watch over and to mortify them, he will be in a continual progress, still gaining ground upon himself; and as he attains to a degree of purity, he will find a nobler flame of life and joy growing up in him. Of this I write with a greater concern and emotion, because I have felt it to be the true, and, indeed, the only joy which runs through a man's heart and life. It is this which has been, for many years, my greatest support. I rejoice daily in it. I feel from it the earnest of that supreme joy which I want and long for ; and I am sure there is nothing else which can afford any true and complete happiness."

SECTION V.

LORD ROCHESTER.

John Wilmot, afterwards earl of Rochester, was born in 1647, at Ditchley, in Oxfordshire. After his education was completed, he travelled into France and Italy; and, at his return, devoted himself to the court, and was in great favor with Charles the Second. He had very early an inclination to intemperance, which he seemed to have totally subdued in his travels; but afterwards falling into dissolute and vicious company, he gave way to his former propensity; and became corrupt in his principles, and depraved in his manners. He lost all sense of religious restraint; and, finding it not convenient to admit the authority of laws which he was resolved not to obey, sheltered his wickedness behind infidelity.

As he excelled in that noisy and licentious merriment which wine excites, his companions eagerly encouraged him in excess, and he willingly indulged it; till, as he confessed to Dr. Burnet, he was for five years together so much inflamed by frequent ebriety, as in no interval to be master of himself.

Thus, in a course of drunken gayety, and gross sensuality, with seasons of study perhaps yet more criminal, with an avowed contempt of all decency and order, a total disregard to every moral, and a resolute denial of every religious obligation, he lived worthless and useless, and blazed out his youth and his health in lavish voluptuousness; till, at the age of one-and-thirty, he had nearly exhausted the fund of life, and had reduced himself to a state of weakness and decay.

At this time he was led to an acquaintance with Dr. Burnet, to whom he laid open with great freedom the tenor of his opinions and the course of his life; and from whom he received such conviction of the reasonableness of moral duty, and the truth of Christianity, as, by the Divine blessing, produced a total change both of his manners and opinions. Some philosophers of the present age will probably suppose, that his contrition and conviction were purely the effects of weakness and low spirits, which scarcely suffer a man to continue in his senses, and certainly not to be master of himself: but Dr. Burnet affirms, that he was "under no such decay as either darkened or weakened his understanding; nor troubled with the spleen or vapors, or under the power of melancholy." In proof of this assertion, the following letter is produced; in which nothing is omitted but some personal compliments to the Doctor:

" WOODSTOCK PARK, Oxfordshire.

" MY MOST HONORED DR. BURNET,

"My spirits and body decay equally together: but weak as I am in person, I shall write you a letter. If God be yet pleased to spare me longer in this world, I hope, by your conversation, to be exalted to such a degree of piety, that the world may see how much I abhor what I so long loved, and how much I glory in repentance, and in God's service. Bestow your prayers upon me, that God would spare me, if it be his good will, to show a true repentance and amendment of life for the time to come; or else, if the Lord please soon to put an end to my worldly being, that he would mercifully accept of my death-bed repentance; and perform that promise he has been pleased to make, that at what time soever a sinner doth repent, he would receive him. Put up these prayers, most dear Doctor, to Almighty God, for your most obedient, languishing servant,

" ROCHESTER.

"June 25, 1680."

Soon after the receipt of this letter, Dr. Burnet visited him. Lord Rochester expressed to him in strong terms, the sense he had of his past life; his sad apprehension for having so offended his Maker and dishonored his Redeemer; the horrors he had gone through; the sincerity of his repentance; and the earnestness with which his mind was turned to call on God, and on his crucified Saviour, to have mercy upon him.

Discoursing one day of the manner of his life from his youth, and bitterly upbraiding himself for his manifold transgressions, he exclaimed, " O blessed God! can such a horrid creature as I am, who have denied thy being, and contemned thy power, be accepted by thee? Can there be mercy and pardon for me? Will God own such a wretch as I am?" About the middle of his sickness, he said : " Shall the unspeakable joys of heaven be conferred on me? O, mighty Saviour! never, but through thy infinite love and satisfaction! O never, but by the purchase of thy blood !"

From the first of his yielding assent to the truths of the Christian religion, his faith seemed sincere and fervent. He highly reprobated " that foolish and absurd philosophy, propagated by the late Hobbes and others, which the world so much admired, and which had undone him, and many persons of the best parts in the nation." His hope of salvation rested solely on the free grace of God, through Jesus Christ. He often prayed that his faith might be strengthened, and cried out, " Lord, I believe, help thou mine unbelief."

He expressed great esteem for the Holy Scriptures, and resolved that if God should spare him, he would frequently read them, and meditate upon them : " for, having spoken to his heart, he acknowledged that all the seeming absurdities and contradictions, which men of corrupt and reprobate judgment supposed to be in them, were vanished: and now that he loved and received the truth, their beauty and excellence appeared."

He frequently implored God's Holy Spirit to comfort and support him, to preserve him from wicked thoughts and suggestions, and from every thing prejudicial to that religious temper of mind with which he was now so happily endued. One night, having been much disturbed by evil imaginations, "I thank God," said he, "I abhor them all. By the power of his grace, which I am sure is sufficient for me, I have overcome them. It is the malice of the devil, because I am rescued from him, that thus troubles me; but the goodness of God frees me from all my spiritual enemies."

He often called for his children, and spoke to them with a warmth of feeling that can scarcely be described. "See," said he to Dr. Burnet, "how good God has been to me, in giving me so many blessings! and yet I have been a most ungracious and unthankful creature!" He expressed much concern for the pious education of his children; and " wished his son might never be a wit; one of those wretched creatures," as he explained it, "who pride themselves in denying the being or the providence of God, and in ridiculing religion; but that he might become an honest and a pious man, by which means only he could be the support and blessing of his family."

He gave a strict charge to the persons in whose custody his papers were, to burn all his obscene and filthy pictures, which were so notoriously scandalous; and all his profane and lewd writings, by which he had so highly offended, and shamed, and blasphemed, that holy religion into which he had been baptized.

He was ready to make restitution, to the utmost of his power, to all persons whom he had injured; and heartily forgave all the wrongs which he had sustained, hoping that he should meet with the like free forgiveness from God.

He expressed a tender concern for his servants, and those who attended him; and earnestly exhorted them to love and fear God. To a gentleman of some character, who came to see him on his death-bed, he said: "O remember that you contemn God no more. He is an avenging God, and will visit you for your sins; and will, I hope, in mercy, touch your conscience, sooner or later, as he has done mine. You and I have been friends and sinners together a great while, and therefore I am the more free with you. We have been all mistaken in our conceits and opinions: our persuasions have been false and groundless: therefore God grant you repentance." And seeing the same gentleman the next day, he said, "Perhaps you were disobliged by my plainness with you yesterday. I spoke the words of truth and soberness:" and striking his hand upon his breast, he added, " I hope God will touch your heart."

He was very desirous to testify to the world his repentance for his past misconduct; and to make every reparation in his power for the mischief, which, by his example and writings, he had occasioned. He sent messages, which well became a dying penitent, to some of his former friends. He strictly enjoined the pious persons who attended him during his last sickness, to publish any thing concerning him that might be a means to reclaim others; praying to God, that, as his life had done much hurt, so his death might do some good. He caused the following solemn declaration to be drawn up, which he signed with his own hand:

" For the benefit of all those whom I may have drawn into sin, by my example and encouragement, I leave to the world this my last declaration, which I deliver in the presence of the GREAT GOD, who knows the secrets of all hearts, and before whom I am preparing to be judged; that, from the bottom of my soul, I detest and abhor the whole course of my former wicked life; that I think I can never sufficiently admire the goodness of God, who has given me a true sense of my pernicious opinions and vile practices, by which I have hitherto lived, without hope, and without God in the world; have been an open enemy to

Jesus Christ, doing the utmost despite to the holy Spirit of Grace ; and that the greatest testimony of my charity to such is, to warn them in the name of God, and as they regard the welfare of their immortal souls, no more to deny his being or his providence, or despise his goodness ; no more to make a mock of sin, or contemn the pure and excellent religion of my ever blessed Redeemer, through whose merits alone, I, one of the greatest of sinners, do yet hope for mercy and forgiveness. Amen.

" J. Rochester.

" Declared and signed in the presence of

" Ann Rochester,
" Robert Parsons."

His sufferings were, at times, very great ; but he did not repine under them. In one of his sharpest fits of pain, looking up to heaven, he said : " God's holy will be done. I bless him for all he does to me."

He expressed his willingness to live, or to die, as it should please Divine Providence. " If," said he, " God should spare me yet a little longer time here, I hope to bring glory to his name, proportionable to the dishonor I have done him, in my whole life past : and particularly, by endeavors to convince others of the danger of their condition, if they continue impenitent ; and by telling them how graciously God has dealt with me."

Near the close of life, he was often heard to pray fervently. He rejoiced in the comfortable persuasion of acceptance with God. A few days before his decease, he said: "I shall now die. But O, what unspeakable glories do I see! What joys, beyond thought or expression, am I sensible of! I am assured of God's mercy to me, through Jesus Christ. O! how I long to die, and to be with my Saviour!"

Thus died, in the thirty-third year of his age, the celebrated earl of Rochester; a memorable instance of the goodness and mercy of God, and of the power of his grace to purify and redeem the most corrupt and obdurate offender. From this case, and from many other instances, the truly penitent sinner, though his sins have been as scarlet or as crimson, may derive hope that God will, even in his greatest extremity, hear his prayers, and accept his repentance: but none should presume on the Divine Mercy, by deferring their amendment till they are brought to the bed of sickness and death. They may suddenly be taken away; they may not have their understanding in the time of illness; they may be deceived with false hopes of recovery; their pains of body may not admit of that state of mind which is proper for the great work of repentance; or, they may have become so hardened by the habits of sin, that they may die, as many have died, without a proper sense of their condition. May the goodness and

forbearance of God lead to repentance and amendment of life, in the time of health! We shall then,
at the approach of death, have no guilty tumults
of mind : no dismal forebodings of the future. We
shall bear our affliction with patience and resignation : and, with joyful hope, commit our spirits
into the hands of a faithful and merciful Creator.

For a further account of Lord Rochester, we
refer the reader to a small volume published by
Dr. Burnet, entitled, "Some Passages of the Life
and Death of John, Earl of Rochester;" "a book,
which," as Dr. Johnson says, "the critic ought to
read for its elegance, the philosopher for its arguments, and the saint for its piety."

CHAPTER VII.

SECTION I.

QUEEN MARY.

MARY, queen of Great Britain, and consort of
King William the Third, was the daughter of
James the Second, and was born in the year 1661.
She appeared to be happily disposed from very
early life, being good and gentle before she was
capable of knowing that it was her duty to be so.
This temper continued with her through the whole
progress of her childhood. She might need instruction, but she wanted no persuasion. And it
is said, that she never once, in the whole course
of her education, gave occasion for reproof. Besides a most amiable sweetness of temper, she possessed great understanding, and a mind cultivated
with useful learning and knowledge.

She was married in the sixteenth year of her age,

to the prince of Orange, and went to reside in Holland, where she conducted herself with so much wisdom and goodness, as to gain universal esteem and affection. But that which was, beyond all comparison, her greatest ornament and possession, was a truly devout and religious temper; which made her look with indifference on the honors and splendor with which she was surrounded, and seek for her highest enjoyment in doing good, in peace of mind, and in the hope of a better life.

In proof of her uncommon merit, we shall here insert a short declaration concerning her, made by her husband, king William, whom she tenderly loved, and who best knew her excellence, and his own great loss in being deprived of her. To Doctor Tenison, who endeavored to comfort him after her death, he observed: "I cannot but grieve, since I have lost a wife, who in seventeen years, never was guilty of an indiscretion. During the whole course of our marriage, I never perceived the least fault in her. She possessed a worth that nobody thoroughly knew but myself."

In the character of lady Russel, we have seen the power and operation of religion on the mind, under some of the darkest clouds of affliction and distress: in the present instance of queen Mary, the virtue and preserving nature of the same Divine principle, is evidenced amidst the magnificence of a court, and the sunshine of worldly prosperity. It is, indeed, a principle of universal agency; adapted to all ranks of men, and to every allotment of Providence; a sure preservative when things are smiling around us, and a sovereign remedy for, or support under, all the calamities of life.

This good queen spent a great part of her time in perusing the holy Scriptures, and other religious books. By a letter to her father, written in early life, in support of the Protestant faith, she appears to have been thoroughly grounded and established in the principles of the Reformation. Bishop Burnet says, that " although he had a high opinion of the princess's good understanding, before he saw this letter, yet the letter surprised him, and gave him an astonishing joy, to see so young a person, all on a sudden, without consulting any one, able to write in so solid and learned a manner."

Her talents and abilities were very conspicuous in all her concerns, and particularly, in the important charge of government. Doctor Tillotson, archbishop of Canterbury, said, that " he was in great admiration at the proofs he knew the queen gave of her knowledge, in the weighty affairs of state, in the king's absence, when the executive part of the government was in her hands."

Her compassion and bounty to the poor and afflicted, and those who stood in need of her liberality, were very eminent, and such as corresponded with her exalted station, and the abundant sources of relief to which she had access. She took care to have a just account both of the worthiness and the necessities of those who were candidates for her liberality; and, in the conducting of her charity, showed as much exactness, attention, and diligence, as if she had no cares of a higher nature. But what crowned all, was her exact conformity to the rule of the Gospel in her munificence: for none knew to whom, or what she gave, but those whom she was obliged to employ in the communication of her bounty.

The piety of this excellent person was a noble support to her under the troubles of life: yet there were some distresses to which it gave a sharper edge. The impieties and blasphemies, the open contempt of religion, and the scorn of virtue, which she heard of from many persons, and from many different parts of the nation, gave her a secret horror; and presented her with so gloomy a prospect, as filled her mind with melancholy reflections. She was very sensibly touched, when she heard that some, who pretended to much zeal for the crown and the revolution, seemed thence to think they had a sort of right to be indulged in their licentiousness and irregularities. She often said, " Can a blessing be expected from such hands, or on anything that must pass through them?"

She had a just esteem for all persons whom she thought truly religious and virtuous; and no other considerations were much regarded by her, when these excellencies were not to be found. Next to open impiety, the want of life in those who pretended to religion, and the deadness and disunion of the Protestants in general, very much affected her; and she often said, with poignant regret: "Can such dry bones live?"

So far was she from entertaining a high opinion of herself, that she had a tender sense of anything that looked like a miscarriage under her conduct; and was afraid lest some mistake of hers might have occasioned it. When difficulties grew too great to be surmounted, and she felt uneasy under them, she made God her refuge; and often said, that "she found herself tranquil, after she had poured forth her soul in prayer." When melancholy events came from the hand of Providence, she said, that "though there was no occasion for complaint or anger, upon these cross occurrences, yet there was just cause of grief, since God's hand was to be seen so particularly in them."

In her brightest seasons, she did not suffer herself to be lulled into security, nor did she withdraw her dependence upon God. In the pleasures of life, she maintained a true indifference as to their continuance; and seemed to think of parting with them, in so easy a manner as plainly showed how little possession they had of her heart.

At one period of her life, she felt such indisposition of body, as induced her to believe that some great sickness was approaching: but, on this occasion, she possessed great quietude and resignation; and said, "that though she did not pray for death, yet she could neither wish nor pray against it. She left that to God, and referred herself to the disposal of Providence. If she did not wish for death, yet she did not fear it."

As this was the state of her mind when she viewed that event at some distance, so she maintained the same composure on its near approach. The end of this extraordinary queen was, indeed, such as might have been expected from the pure and exemplary life she had lived. When she was first informed of the danger to be apprehended from her disorder, (which was the small-pox,) she calmly said: "I have been instructed how very hazardous a thing it is, to rely upon a death-bed repentance: I am not now to begin the great work of preparing for death; and, I praise God, I am not afraid of it." Under the weight of her disorder, which was very trying to nature, she appeared to feel no inward depression or discouragement of mind. A willingness to die, and an entire resignation to the will of God, accompanied her to the closing scene; in the near approach of which she declared, that "she experienced the joys of a good conscience, and the power of religion giving her supports, which even the last agonies could not shake." Thus died this most excellent princess; and, no doubt, passed from an earthly to a heavenly crown, "a crown of glory that shall never fade away."

The contemplation of so peaceful and happy conclusions of life, as this, and others which are mentioned in the present work, is sufficient, at times, to elevate the soul, and to make all the glories and enjoyments of this transient scene sink into nothing. Ah! these are favored, precious moments, when the Divine Power of Religion breaks in upon us, dissolves the enchantment of the world, dissipates the mist of vain doubts and speculation, and raises a fervent aspiration, that whatever may be our allotment through life, we may die the death of the righteous, and the love of God be our portion for ever!

SECTION II.

BOERHAAVE.

Herman Boerhaave, one of the greatest physicians, and best of men, was born in Holland, in the year 1668. This illustrious person, whose name has been spread throughout the world, and who left at his death above two hundred thousand pounds sterling, was, at his first setting out in life, obliged to teach the mathematics to obtain a necessary support. His abilities, industry, and great merit, soon gained him friends, placed him in easy circumstances, and enabled him to be bountiful to others.

The knowledge and learning of this great man, however uncommon, hold in his character but the second place; his virtue was yet much more uncommon than his literary attainments. He was an admirable example of temperance, fortitude, humility, and devotion. His piety, and profound sense of his dependence on God, were the basis of all his virtues, and the principle of his whole conduct. He was too sensible of his weakness to ascribe anything to himself, or to conceive that he could subdue passion, or withstand temptation by his own natural power: he attributed every good thought and every laudable action to the Father of Goodness.

Being once asked by a friend, who had often admired his patience under great provocations, whether he had ever been under the influence of anger, and by what means he had so entirely suppressed that impetuous and ungovernable passion; he answered, with the utmost frankness and sincerity, that he was naturally quick of resentment, but that he had, by daily prayer and meditation, at length attained to this mastery over himself.

As soon as he rose in the morning, it was, through life, his daily practice, to retire for an hour for private prayer and meditation. This, he often told his friends gave him spirit and vigor in the business of the day; and this he therefore commended as the best rule of life: for nothing, he knew, can support the soul in all distresses, but confidence in the Supreme Being; nor can a steady and rational magnanimity flow from any other source than a consciousness of the Divine favor.

He asserted, on all occasions, the Divine authority of the Holy Scriptures. The excellence of the Christian religion was the frequent subject of his conversation. A strict obedience to the doctrine, and a diligent imitation of the example, of our blessed Saviour, he often declared to be the foundation of true tranquility. He was liberal to the distressed, but without ostentation. He often obliged his friends in such a manner, that they knew not, unless by accident, to whom they were indebted. He was condescending to all, and particularly attentive in his profession. He used to say, that the life of a patient, if trifled with or neglected, would one day be required at the hand of the physician. He called the poor his best patients: for God, said he, is their paymaster. In conversation, he was cheerful and instructive; and desirous of promoting every valuable end of social intercourse. He never regarded calumny and detraction, (for Boerhaave himself had enemies,) nor ever thought it necessary to confute them. "They are sparks," said he, "which if you do not blow them, will go out of themselves. The surest remedy against scandal, is, to live it down by perseverance in well-doing; and by praying to God, that he would cure the distempered minds of those who traduce and injure us."

About the middle of the year 1737, he felt the first approaches of that lingering disorder, which at length brought him to the grave. During this afflictive illness, his constancy and firmness did not forsake him. He neither intermitted the necessary cares of life, nor forgot the proper preparations for death.

He related to a friend, with great concern, that once his patience so far gave way to extremity of pain, that, after having lain fifteen hours in exquisite tortures, he prayed to God that he might be set free by death. His friend, by way of consolation, answered, that he thought such wishes, when forced by continued and excessive torments, unavoidable in the present state of human nature; that the best men, even Job himself, were not able to refrain from such starts of impatience. This he did not deny, but said, "He that loves God, ought to think nothing desirable but what is most pleasing to the Supreme Goodness."

Such were his sentiments, and such his conduct, in this state of weakness and pain. As death advanced nearer, he was so far from terror or confusion, that he seemed even less sensible of pain, and more cheerful under his torments. He died, much honored and lamented, in the 70th year of his age.

In contemplating the character of this excellent man, what strikes us most is, that far from being made impious by philosophy, or vain by knowledge or by virtue, he ascribed all his abilities to the bounty, and all his goodness to the grace of God. "May his example," says Dr. Johnson, his biographer, "extend its influence to his admirers and followers! May those who study his writings, imitate his life; and those who endeavor after his knowledge, aspire likewise to his piety!"

SECTION III.

JOSEPH ADDISON.

Joseph Addison, a celebrated English writer, was born at Milston, in Wiltshire, in the year 1672. About the age of fifteen, he was entered at Queen's college, Oxford, where, by his fine parts and great application, he made a surprising proficiency in classical learning. Before he left the university, he was warmly solicited to enter into orders; and he once resolved to do so: but his great modesty, and an uncommonly delicate sense of the importance of the sacred function, made him afterwards alter his resolution.

He was highly respected by many of the greatest, and the most learned of his contemporaries. He travelled into Italy, where he made many useful observations, and prepared materials for some of his literary works. On his return to England, he was chosen one of the lords commissioners for trade. In 1709, he was appointed secretary to the lord lieutenant of Ireland; and in 1717, was advanced to the high office of secretary of state.

His writings have been of great use to the world; and his "Evidences of the Christian Religion," not the least so. Dr. Johnson, in delineating his character, as a writer, gives the following amiable picture of him: "He employed wit on the side of virtue and religion. He not only made the proper use of wit himself, but taught it to others; and, from his time, it has been generally subservient to the cause of reason and truth. He has dissipated the prejudice that had long connected cheerfulness with vice, and easiness of manners with laxity of principles. He has restored virtue to its dignity, and taught innocence not to be ashamed. This is an elevation of literary character above all Greek, above all Roman fame. As a teacher of wisdom, he may be confidently followed. His religion has nothing in it enthusiastic or superstitious: he appears neither weakly credulous, nor wantonly sceptical: his morality is neither dangerously lax, nor impracticably rigid. All the enchantment of fancy, and all the cogency of argument are employed to recommend to the reader his real interest, the care of pleasing the Author of his being."

Of his integrity in discharging the duties of his office, there is a striking proof recorded. When he was secretary in Ireland, he had materially promoted the interest of an individual, who offered him, in return, a bank-note of three hundred pounds, and a diamond ring of the same value. These he strenuously refused to accept, and wrote to the person as follows: "And now, sir, believe me, when I assure you, I never did, nor ever will, on any pretence whatever, take more than the stated and customary fees of my office. I might keep the contrary practice concealed from the world, were I capable of it; but I could not from myself! and I hope I shall always fear the reproaches of my own heart more than those of all mankind."

A mind conscious of its own uprightness, and humbly trusting in the goodness of God, has the best ground to look forward with complacency towards another life. The following lines of Addison are sweetly expressive of the peace and pleasure which he enjoyed, in contemplating his future existence: "The prospect of a future state is the secret comfort and refreshment of my soul. It is that which makes nature look cheerful about me; it doubles all my pleasures, and supports me under all my afflictions. I can look at disappointments and misfortunes, pain and sickness, death itself, with indifference, so long as I keep in view the pleasures of eternity, and the state of being in which there will be no fears nor apprehensions, pains or sorrows."

The virtue of this excellent man shone brightest at the point of death. After a long and manly, but vain strugg'e with his distempers, he dismissed his physicians, and with them all hopes of life; but with his hopes of life he dismissed not his concern for the living. He sent for Lord Warwick, a youth, nearly related to him, and finely accomplished, but irregular in conduct and principle; on whom his pious instructions and example had not produced the desired effect. Lord Warwick came; but life now glimmering in the socket, the dying friend was silent. After a decent and proper pause, the youth said: "Dear sir! you sent for me: I believe, and hope you have some commands: I shall hold them most dear." May the reader not only feel the reply, but retain its impression! Forcibly grasping the youth's hand, Addison softly said: "See in what peace a Christian can die!" He spoke with difficulty, and soon expired. Through Divine grace, how great is man! Through Divine mercy, how stingless death!

SECTION IV.

ANN BAYNARD.

Ann Baynard was descended from an ancient and respectable family, and was born in the year 1672. She possessed strong powers of mind; understood the learned languages; and made considerable acquisitions in the arts and sciences. She took great delight in study, and seemed to know no bounds in the pursuit of learning and knowledge. But when she formed a serious estimate of things, and compared the highest accomplishments of this life, with the possession of Divine peace, and the hope of eternal happiness, her extreme love of learning, and of the distinctions that accompany it, abated. She then declared, that "she counted all things but loss, in comparison of the excellence of the knowledge of Christ Jesus her Lord; and that human learning is worth but little, unless it serve as a handmaid to the knowledge of Christ revealed in the Gospel, as our only Lord and Saviour." "What avails," said she, "Solomon's skill in the works of nature, if by it we are not brought to see the God of nature? What advantage is it to be so learned in astronomy, or the knowledge of the heavens, that we can foretell things to come, if we never study, by our holy practice, to arrive at the blessed regions? What advantage is it, to be so skilful in arithmetic, that we can divide and subdivide to the smallest fraction, if, as God has revealed unto us in his holy word, we do not learn to number our days, and apply our hearts to wisdom? What advantage is it, for a physician to know how to prevent or cure the disease of the body, if he knows not where to find the balm of Gilead, the wine and oil of the Good Samaritan, the Lord Jesus Christ, to pour into the wounds of his own soul?"

The mind of this excellent woman was much raised above the vanities of this world, its gayeties and splendor. Having experienced the happiness of a devout and pious life, she had no relish for pleasures of a different nature. She had a high veneration for the Author of her being, and made it her great business to promote his honor and glory. She observed, with deep concern, the errors, follies, and vices of the age; and was not only importunate in her intercessions for the good of the world, but solicitous to benefit the souls of those with whom she conversed, by friendly reproof, good counsel, or pious discourse. But the period of her life and labors was of short duration; for she was only twenty-five years of age when she died.

SECTION V.

ELIZABETH ROWE.

Elizabeth Rowe, the daughter of a very respectable dissenting minister, was born at Ilchester, in Somersetshire, in the year 1674. She discovered early symptoms of fine parts: and as her strongest bent was to poetry, she began to write verses at twelve years of age. She possessed uncommon elegance of mind, and exquisite sensibility. She also manifested a pious and devout disposition, even when she was very young. It was a peculiar happiness to her, that, early in life, she enjoyed the friendship of the pious Bishop Ken; at whose request she wrote a paraphrase on the thirty-eighth chapter of Job.

Her shining merit, and various accomplishments, procured her many admirers: but the person who obtained her in marriage, was Thomas Rowe, a gentleman of uncommon parts and learning, and of great worth. The connection proved happy, but was of short duration. The husband of this excellent woman died of a consumption at twenty-eight years of age, having lived with his amiable consort scarcely five years. The elegy which she composed upon his death, is one of her best poems.

After the decease of her husband, the world appeared in her view with less attraction than ever. She retired to her estate at Frome, where she spent the remainder of her days. In this retreat, the religious temper of her mind increased; and here she wrote the greater part of her works. Her book, entitled "Devout Exercises of the Heart, in Meditation and Soliloquy, Praise and Prayer," has been much read and commended. This work she sealed up, and directed it to be delivered to Dr. Watts, after her decease; with a letter to him, in which she gives some account both of the work and of herself. The letter contains so much of a devout and Christian spirit, that we shall insert a part of it in this collection.

"The 'Reflections' were occasionally written, and only for my own improvement; but I am not without hope that they may have the same salutary effect on some pious minds, as reading the experience of others has had on my own soul. The experimental part of religion has generally a greater influence than the theory of it; and if, when I am sleeping in the dust, these soliloquies should kindle a flame of Divine love, even in the heart of the lowest and most despised Christian, be the glory given to the great Spring of all grace and benignity!

"I have now done with mortal things, and all to come is vast eternity! Eternity! how transporting is the sound! As long as God exists, my being and happiness are, I doubt not, secure. These unbounded desires, which the wide creation cannot limit, shall be satisfied for ever. I shall drink at the fountain-head of pleasure, and be refreshed with the emanations of original life and joy. I shall hear the voice of uncreated harmony, speaking peace and ineffable consolation to my soul.

"I expect eternal life, not as a reward of merit, but as a pure act of bounty. Detesting myself in every view I can take, I fly to the righteousness and atonement of my great Redeemer, for pardon and salvation: this is my only consolation and hope. Enter not into judgment, O Lord, with thy servant; for in thy sight shall no flesh be justified. Through the blood of the Lamb, I hope for an entire victory over the last enemy; and that, before this comes to you, I shall have reached the celestial heights; and, while you are reading these lines, I shall be adoring before the throne of God; where faith shall be turned into vision, and these languishing desires satisfied with the full fruition of immortal love. Amen."

SECTION VI.

DOCTOR WATTS.

Isaac Watts, a learned and eminent dissenting minister, was born at Southampton, in the year 1674, of parents who were distinguished by their piety and virtue. He possessed uncommon genius, and gave early proofs of it. He received a very liberal education, which was rendered highly beneficial to him, by his own unwearied efforts to improve himself. After the most serious deliberation, he determined to devote his life to the ministry; of the importance of which office he had a deep and awful sense. He labored very diligently to promote the instruction and happiness of the people under his care: and, by his Christian conduct and amiable disposition, greatly endeared himself to them.

Soon after he had undertaken the pastoral office, his health sustained a severe shock, by a painful and dangerous illness; from which he recovered very slowly. But in the year 1712, he was afflicted with a violent fever, that entirely broke his constitution, and left such weakness upon his nerves as continued with him, in some measure, to the day of his death.

For four years, he was wholly prevented from discharging the public offices of his station. Though this long interval of sickness was, no doubt, very trying to his active mind, yet it proved ultimately a blessing; for it drew upon him the particular notice of Sir Thomas Abney, a very pious and worthy man, who, from motives of friendship, invited him into his family; in which he continued to the end of his life; and, for the long space of thirty-six years, was treated with uniform kindness, attention, and respect.

Dr. Johnson's judicious account of Watts, exhibits him, both as a man and a writer, in a very pleasing light. We shall select from it a few striking passages:

"This excellent man was, by his natural temper, quick of resentment; but, by his established and habitual practice, he was gentle, modest, and inoffensive. His tenderness appeared in his attention to children, and to the poor. To the poor, while he lived in the family of his friend, he allowed the third part of his annual revenue; and for children, he condescended to lay aside the scholar, the philosopher, and the wit, to write little poems of devotion, and systems of instruction adapted to their wants and capacities, from the dawn of reason through its gradations of advance in the morning of life.

"Few men have left behind them such purity of character, or such monuments of laborious piety.

He has provided instruction for all ages, from those who are lisping their first lessons, to the enlightened readers of Malbranche and Locke. His 'Improvement of the Mind,' is a work in the highest degree useful and pleasing. Whatever he took in hand was, by his incessant solicitude for souls, converted to theology. As piety predominated in his mind, it is diffused over his works. Under his direction it may be truly said, that philosophy is subservient to evangelical instruction: it is difficult to read a page without learning, or at least, wishing to be better."

The virtue of this good man eminently appeared, in the happy state of his mind, under great pains and weakness of body, and in the improvement which he derived from them. Of those seasons of affliction, he says, with a truly elevated mind and thankful heart: "I am not afraid to let the world know, that amidst the sinkings of life and nature, Christianity and the Gospel were my support. Amidst all the violence of my distemper, and the tiresome months of it, I thank God, I never lost sight of reason or religion, though sometimes I had much difficulty to preserve the machine of animal nature in such order, as regularly to exercise either the man or the Christian."

The sweet peace of conscience he enjoyed, under these trying circumstances, and the rational and Christian foundation of his hope and trust in the Divine Goodness, are beautifully and justly expressed by him in the following lines:

> " Yet, gracious God ! amid these storms of nature,
> Thine eyes behold a sweet and sacred calm
> Reign through the realms of conscience: all within
> Lies peaceful, all composed. 'Tis wondrous Grace
> Keeps off thy terrors from this humble bosom;
> Though stain'd with sins and follies, yet serene
> In penitential peace and cheerful hope,
> Sprinkled and guarded with atoning blood.
> Thy vital smiles, amidst this desolation,
> Like heav'nly sunbeams, hid behind the clouds,
> Break out in happy moments, with bright radiance
> Cleaving the gloom ; the fair celestial light
> Softens and gilds the horrors of the storm,
> And richest cordials to the heart conveys.

> " O glorious solace of immense distress,
> A conscience and a God ! This is my rock
> Of firm support, my shield of sure defence
> Against infernal arrows. Rise, my soul !
> Put on thy courage : here's the living spring
> Of joys divinely sweet and ever new,
> A peaceful conscience, and a smiling Heav'n.

> " My God, permit a creeping worm to say,
> Thy Spirit knows I love thee !—Worthless wretch,
> To dare to love a God !—But grace requires,
> And grace accepts. Thou seest my lab'ring soul.
> Weak as my zeal is, yet my zeal is true;
> It bears the trying furnace. Love divine
> Constrains me : I am thine. Incarnate Love
> Has seized, and holds me in almighty arms !
> Here's my salvation, my eternal hope—
> Amidst the wreck of worlds and dying nature,
> I am the Lord's, and he's for ever mine !"

When his sufferings were, in some degree, alleviated, what excellent effects were produced in his mind! How was his heart enlarged with love and gratitude to God! and in what pathetic language did he pour out his spirit!

> "Almighty Power, I love thee! blissful name,
> My healer God! and may my inmost heart
> Love and adore for ever! O 'tis good
> To wait submissive at thy holy throne,
> To leave petitions at thy feet, and bear
> Thy frowns and silence with a patient soul!
> The hand of mercy is not short to save,
> Nor is the ear of heavenly pity deaf
> To mortal cries. It noticed all my groans,
> And sighs, and long complaints, with wise delay,
> Though painful to the suff'rer; and thy hand
> In proper moment brought desired relief."

And now, how amiable does he appear, when the shadows of the evening were stretching over him! Two or three years before his decease, the active and sprightly powers of his nature gradually failed; yet his trust in God, through Jesus the Mediator, remained unshaken to the last. He was heard to say: "I bless God I can lie down with comfort at night, not being solicitous whether I awake in this world or another." And again: "I should be glad to read more; yet not in order to be further confirmed in the truth of the Christian religion, or in the truth of its promises; for I believe them enough to venture an eternity upon them."

When he was almost worn out, and broken down

by his infirmities, he said, in conversation with a friend; "I remember an aged minister used to observe, that 'the most learned and knowing Christians, when they come to die, have only the same plain promises of the gospel for their support, as the common and unlearned:' and so, I find it. It is the plain promises of the gospel that are my support; and, I bless God, they are plain promises, that do not require much labor and pains to understand them."

At times, when he found his spirit tending to impatience, and ready to complain that he could only lead a mere animal life, he would check himself thus: "The business of a Christian is, to bear the will of God, as well as to do it. If I were in health, I ought to be doing it, and now it is my duty to bear it. The best thing in obedience, is a regard to the will of God; and the way to that is, to have our inclinations and aversions as much mortified as we can."

With so calm and peaceful a mind, so blessed and lively a hope, did the resigned servant of Christ wait for his Master's summons. He quietly expired in the seventy-fifth year of his age.

11

CHAPTER VIII.

SECTION I.

LADY ELIZABETH HASTINGS.

IN the life, sufferings, and death, of Lady Elizabeth Hastings, we have a lively instance of the power and support of religion.

An ingenuous temper, a quickness of understanding, a benevolent spirit, a flexibility of nature, and a solemn sense of Divine things, were observable in her tender age; and, in the dangerous ascent of life, her feet were guided and preserved in the paths of rectitude and goodness; so that she was not only free from the stain of vice in her rising years, but superior to the world, and its vain and trifling amusements. Through the whole course of her time, her lamp shone brightly; and in mature age, diffused its light and influence in a wide extent around her.

It appears that the great aim of her life was, to promote the glory of God, and the welfare of men, keeping her talents, extensive fortune, and other means of doing good, continually employed for the benefit of her fellow-creatures. Of all her cares, a most especial one was that of the stranger, the fatherless, and the widow; the needy, and him that had no helper; the lame, the halt, and the blind. These objects excited her most tender compassion. She participated in their sufferings; she often conversed with them; and inquired into their history, with great condescension. She studied their particular cases, and put them in the way of improving their condition. She often visited them in sickness, bore the expenses of it; and, no doubt, endeavored to cheer and encourage them under all the apparent hardships of their allotment.

The following character of this noble-minded woman, was drawn by the hand of an eminent writer: " Her countenance was the lively picture of her mind, which was the seat of honor, truth, compassion, knowledge, and innocence. In the midst of the most ample fortune, and the veneration of all that beheld and knew her, without the least affectation she devoted herself to retirement, to the contemplation of her own being, and of that Supreme Power which bestowed it. Without the learning of schools, or knowledge of a long course of arguments, she went on in an uninterrupted course of piety and virtue; and added to the severity and privacy of the last age, all the freedom and ease of this. The language and mien of a court she was possessed of in a high degree; but the simplicity and humble thoughts of a cottage, were her more welcome entertainments. She was a female philosopher, who did not only live up to the resignation of the most retired lives of the ancient sages, but also to the schemes and plans which they thought beautiful, though inimitable. This lady was the most exact economist, without appearing busy; the most strictly virtuous, without tasting the praise of it; and shunned applause with as much industry as others do reproach."

Towards the close of life, she experienced great bodily affliction, having a cancer in the breast, for which she underwent an amputation. But in all her sufferings from this cause, and even under the trying operation, her religious fortitude and serenity of mind did not forsake her. The resignation of her spirit to the dispensations of Divine Providence, is strongly marked by the following expressions, which dropped from her during the course of this painful distemper: "I would not wish to be out of my present situation, for all the world; nor exchange it for any other, at any price."

The night subsequent to the operation did not afford her much sleep, but it was a night of celestial peace; a time of thanksgiving to her God, for the visible demonstration of his power in and about her; for his stretched-out arm in her great deliverance; for the bountiful provisions he had made for all the wants of her soul and body; and, in a word, 'for all his blessings conferred upon her.

She was, sooner than expected, restored to a comfortable state of health, and to that life of charity and beneficence, which was the joy of her heart: but the disorder, repressed only for a time, appeared again with new malignity, and, at length, put a period to all her sorrows. Her lamp and her life were, however, to be extinguished together: she was pious and beneficent to the last.

A short time before her departure, impressed with a strong sense of Divine Goodness, she broke out, with a raised accent, in the following manner: "Lord! what is it that I see? O, the greatness of the glory that is revealed in me! that is before me!" So joyful appears to have been her entrance into the kingdom of her Lord and Saviour. She died in the year 1740.

The truly religious, whose evidences of a blessed futurity are clear, rational, and well-founded, have, at times, in their journey through life, a tide of hope and joy springing up in their minds, beyond expression; a felicity more moving and satisfactory than any can imagine, but they who have, in some degree, experienced it. And when they are just entering upon the promised land, they are sometimes favored to have the splendor of the eternal day dawn upon them, and to shine as through the breaches of their shattered bodies; raising in their spirits such an earnest of happiness, such foretastes of joy, as enable them to pass through the valley of death in peace and triumph. What a rich reward for all the crosses and conflicts of this probationary scene! and how animating a source of encouragement, during our pilgrimage, to rise above, and look beyond, all the troubles of time!

SECTION II.

H. HOUSMAN.

THERE are few greater instances of the happy
power of religion on the mind, than that which was
exhibited by an excellent and pious woman of the
name of Housman, when she drew near the close
of life.

She was born at Kidderminster, of religious
parents, who early instructed her in the duties of
religion. By her diary, it appears she was brought
under lively impressions of Divine things, at thirteen years of age. From 1711, when her diary
begins, to 1735, the time of her death, her life
seems to have been a circumspect walking in the
fear of God. The following account of her last
illness and death was drawn up by a person who
attended her throughout.

From the time of her first seizure, she was exercised with very violent pains, without any intermis-
sion, till her death; such as, she would often say,
she thought she could not have borne: "but," said
she, "God is good; verily he is good to me! I
have found him a good and gracious God to me all
my days."

When recovering from extreme pain, she said: "God is good; I have found him so; and though he slay me, yet I will trust in him. These pains make me love my Lord Jesus the better. O they put me in mind of what he suffered, to purchase salvation for my poor soul! Why for me, Lord! why for me, the greatest of sinners? Why for me, who so long refused the rich offers of thy grace, and the kind invitations of the gospel? How many helps and means have I enjoyed more than many others; yea, above most! I had a religious father and mother; and I had access to a valuable minister, to whom I could often and freely open my mind. I have lived in a golden age. I have lived in peaceable times, and have enjoyed great advantages and helps for communion with God, and the peace of my own mind: for which I owe my gracious God and Father more praises than words can express. Bless the Lord, O my soul, and all that is within me bless his holy name! Bless the Lord, O my soul, and forget not all, or any, of his benefits!"

When any were weeping and mourning over her, she would say: "Weep not for me; it is the will of God; therefore be content. If it may be for his honor and glory, he will spare me a little longer; if not, I am wholly resigned to the will of God. I am content to stay here, as long as he has any thing for me to do, or to suffer; and I am willing to go, if it be my Father's good pleasure.

Therefore be content, and say, 'It is the Lord; let him do what seemeth to him good.'"

To a person who came to see her, she said: "Cousin, I think I shall die: and now, what a comfort it is, that I am not afraid of death! The blood of Christ cleanses me from all sin. But mistake me not; there must be a life and conversation agreeable to the gospel, or else our faith in Christ is a dead faith. Secure Christ for your friend; set not your heart on things below: riches and honors, and what the world calls pleasures, are all fading, perishing things." She then threw out her hand, and said: "O, if I had thousands and ten thousands of gold and silver lying by me, what could they do for me now I am dying? Take the advice of a departing friend who wishes you well. Do not set your affections on riches, or on any thing here below. Remember, death will come in a little while, whether you are ready or unready, willing or unwilling. I commend you to God. I hope, in a short time, we shall meet again in heaven, that place of perfect rest, peace, and happiness."

The whole time of her sickness, she was in a cheerful, thankful frame of mind. When she was cold, and had something warm given to her, she often said: "Blessed be God for all his mercies; and for this comfort in my affliction." On her attendant's warming a piece of flannel, and putting it round her cold hands, she thanked her for it, and said: "O, how many mercies I have! I want

11*

for nothing. Here is every thing I can wish for.
I can say, I never wanted any good thing. I wish
only for a tranquil passage to glory. It was free
Grace that plucked me from the very brink of hell;
and it is the power of Divine Grace, that has supported me through the whole of my life. Hitherto
I can say, the Lord is gracious. He has been very
merciful to me, in sustaining me under all my trials.
The Lord brings affliction, but it is not because he
delights to afflict his children : it is at all times for
our profit. I can say, it has been good for me to
be afflicted; it has enabled me to discern things,
which, when I was in health, I could not perceive.
It has made me see more of the vanity and emptiness of this world, and all its transient comforts;
for, at best, they are but vanity. I can say from
my own experience, I have found them to be so
many a time."

To her husband, the day before she died, she
said : " My dear, I think I am going apace; and I
hope you will be satisfied, because it is the will of
God. You have at all times been very loving and
good to me ; and I thank you for it kindly: and
now I desire you freely to resign me to God. If
God sees it best to prolong my stay here upon
earth, I am willing to stay; or, if he sees it best to
take me to himself, I am willing to go. I am willing to be, and to bear, what may be most for his
glory."

The evening before she died, she found death

stealing upon her; and, feeling her own pulse, said: "Well, it will be but a little while before my work in this world will be finished. Then I shall have done with prayer. My whole employment in heaven will be praise and love. Here, I love God but faintly, yet, I hope, sincerely; but there it will be perfectly. I shall behold his face in righteousness; for I am thy servant, Lord! bought with blood, with precious blood. Christ died to purchase the life of my soul. A little while, and then I shall be singing that sweet song, 'Blessing, and honor, and glory, and power, be unto HIM that sitteth upon the throne, and to the Lamb for ever and ever.'"

With smiles on her face, and transports of joy she often said: "Come, Lord Jesus, come quickly! Why tarry the wheels of thy chariot? O, blessed convoy! come and fetch my soul, to dwell with God, and Christ, and perfect spirits for ever and ever. When I join that blessed society above, my pleasures will never end. O, the glory that shall be set on the head of faith and love!"

A few minutes before her departure, finding herself going, she desired to be lifted up. When this was done, she cheerfully said: "Farewell sin! farewell pains!" and so finished her course with joy.

SECTION III.

DOCTOR DODDRIDGE.

PHILIP DODDRIDGE was born in London, in the year 1702. His parents, who were persons of great worth, brought him up in an early knowledge of religion : but he had the misfortune to lose them before he was fourteen years old. This circumstance excited in his mind very serious reflections, which, however, were not wholly of a gloomy nature; for he expressed a devout, and even a cheerful trust in the protection of the God of Mercies, the universal Parent of mankind.

He diligently improved his time, and was anxious to be daily advancing in knowledge, piety, virtue, and usefulness. He possessed strong powers of mind, and, by unwearied application, acquired a large fund of sound and elegant learning. His publications, which are chiefly on religious subjects, have been eminently useful to the world. By his literary acquisitions, his amiable disposition, and his desire to imbue the young mind with knowledge and virtue, he was qualified, in a peculiar manner, to become the instructor of youth; and for many years he superintended a very re-

spectable academy. As the pastor of a congregation, he manifested a sincere and zealous regard for
the happiness of the people under his care, by
whom he was greatly honored and beloved.

He possessed many virtues; but the prime and
leading feature of his soul, was devotion. He was
very solicitous to preserve and cultivate an habitual
sense of the Supreme Being; to maintain and increase the ardor of religion in his heart; and to
prepare himself, by devout exercises, for the important labors of his station. Nor was it to his
secret retirements that his piety was limited: it
was manifested in every part of the day, and appeared in his usual intercourse with men. In the
little vacancies of time which occur to the busiest
of mankind, he was frequently lifting up his soul to
God. When he lectured on philosophy, history,
anatomy, or other subjects not immediately theo-
logical, he would endeavor to graft some religious
instructions upon them, that he might raise the
minds of his pupils to devotion, as well as to knowledge; and in his visits to his people, the Christian
friend and minister were united.

The piety of Dr. Doddridge was accompanied
with the warmest benevolence to his fellow-creatures. No one could more strongly feel that the
love of God must be united with love to man.
Nor was this a principle that rested in kind wishes,
and pathetic feelings for the happiness of others,
but it was manifested in the most active exertions

for their welfare. No scheme of doing good was ever suggested to him, into which he did not enter with ardor. But the generosity of his mind was the most displayed, when any plans of propagating religion, and of spreading the gospel among those who were strangers to it, were proposed. In everything of this kind, he was always ready to take the lead, and was ardent in endeavoring to inspire his friends with the same spirit.

He was of a weak and delicate bodily constitution; and a severe cold which he caught about the forty-eighth year of his age, brought on a consumption of the lungs. The nearer he approached to his dissolution, the more plainly was observed his continual improvement in a spiritual and heavenly temper. Indeed, he seemed to have risen above the world, and to be daily breathing after immortality. This disposition of his mind was ardently expressed in several of his letters; and it is manifest from his will, which was made at this time, and is prefaced in the following language: "Whereas it is customary on these occasions, to begin with commending the soul into the hands of God, through Christ; I do it, not in mere form, but with sincerity and joy; esteeming it my greatest happiness, that I am taught and encouraged to do it, by that glorious gospel, which, having most assuredly believed it, I have spent my life in preaching to others; and which I esteem an infinitely greater treasure than all my little worldly store, or possessions ten thousand times greater than mine."

Having made trial of the waters of Bristol, and his health still continuing more and more to decline, he was advised by his physicians and friends, as the last resort in so threatening a disorder, to remove to a warmer climate. He accordingly went to Lisbon. His resignation to the Divine disposal is strongly marked in a letter, which he wrote soon after his arrival there. After mentioning his great weakness and danger, he added :

"Nevertheless, I bless God, the most undisturbed serenity continues in my mind, and my strength holds proportion to my day. I still hope and trust in God, and joyfully acquiesce in all he may do with me. When you see my dear friends of the congregation, inform them of my circumstances, and assure them, that I cheerfully submit myself to God. If I desire life may be restored, it is chiefly that it may be employed in serving Christ among them. I am enabled, by faith, to look upon death as an enemy that shall be destroyed ; and can cheerfully leave my dear Mrs. Doddrige a widow in a strange land, if such be the appointment of our Heavenly Father. I hope I have done my duty; and the Lord do as seemeth good in his sight."

Change of climate did not produce the desired effect, and Dr. Doddridge continued gradually to weaken, till death put a period to his afflictions. In his last hours he preserved the same calmness, vigor, and joy of mind, which he had felt and expressed through the whole of his illness. The only pain he had in the thought of dying, was the fear of that grief and distress which his wife would suffer from his removal. To his children, his congregation, and his friends in general, he desired to be remembered in the most affectionate manner; nor did he, in the effusions of his pious benevolence, forget the family where he lodged, or his own servant. Many devout sentiments and aspirations were uttered by him: but the heart of his wife was too much affected with his approaching change, to be able to recollect them distinctly. Though he died in a foreign land, and, in a certain sense, among strangers, his decease was embalmed with many tears.*

* A judicious life of this excellent man, written by Dr. Kippis, is prefixed to the first volume of Dr. Doddridge's Family Expositor.

CHAPTER IX.

Louis, Duke of Orleans—Soame Jenyns—Lord Lyttelton
—Jonas Hanway—Anthony Benezet—James Hervey—
Altamont, or the Death of the Libertine.

SECTION I.

LOUIS, DUKE OF ORLEANS.

Louis, duke of Orleans, first prince of the blood royal of France, and highly distinguished for piety and learning, was born at Versailles, in the year 1703. He was the son of Philip, duke of Orleans, regent of France, and of Mary Frances of Bourbon. He discovered, in his very childhood, a reverence for religion, a shining genius, and an enlarged understanding. At an early age he became sensible of the vanity of titles, pre-eminence, and all the splendor of life. He proposed to himself a new mode of conduct, which he afterwards pursued, dividing his time between the duties peculiar to his rank, the exercises of a Christian, and the studies which improve the mind. He was, in every respect, a pattern of self-denial, of piety, and of virtue.

His religion was not merely contemplative; for he possessed a most extensive charity, and an enlightened zeal for the public good. The indigent of every age, sex, and condition, excited his compassionate regard. He daily heard their complaints in one of the halls of the convent of St. Genevieve; he sympathized with them; he alleviated their distresses. When it was not in his power to dismiss them entirely satisfied, his heart seemed to grant what necessity obliged him to refuse. It is hardly to be imagined what sums this pious prince expended, in placing children for education in colleges and nunneries, in portioning young women, endowing nuns, putting boys apprentices, or purchasing for them their freedom; in setting up unfortunate tradesmen in business again, and preventing the ruin of others; in restoring and supporting noblemen's families; in relieving the sick, and paying surgeons for their attendance on them. Very often, accompanied by a single servant, he sought after poor persons, in chambers and garrets, and kindly administered to their wants. He made great improvements in physic, agriculture, arts, and manufactures. He purchased, and published, a variety of useful remedies. His gardens were filled with medicinal plants of all sorts, brought from the most distant climates.

The delight he found in piety and devotion, he

used thus to express: "I know, by experience, that sublunary grandeur and sublunary pleasure are delusive and vain; and are always infinitely below the conceptions we form of them: but, on the contrary, such happiness, and such complacence may be found in devotion and piety, as the sensual mind has no idea of."

In his last illness, perceiving that death was approaching, he prepared for it with the greatest fortitude and composure; and spoke of it as of the demise of another person. In his will he expatiated, in the most pathetic manner, on his belief in the resurrection.

At the concluding period of life, his mind seemed filled with the love of God; and he implored, with the utmost earnestness, the Divine blessing for his son, the duke of Chartres. "I have a son," said he to the minister who attended him, "whom I am going to commend to the all-perfect Being. I entreat God that his natural virtues may become Christian graces; that the qualities which gain him esteem, may be serviceable to his salvation; that his love for the king, and his love for me, may be the blossoms of that immortal charity, which the holy spirits and blessed angels enjoy."

Thus died this truly Christian prince, in the forty-ninth year of his age.

SECTION II.

SOAME JENYNS.

Soame Jenyns was born in London, in the year 1704. He was carefully educated in his father's house, till he went to the university of Cambridge, where he studied very diligently for several years. In 1741, he represented Cambridge in Parliament; where he continued to sit, chiefly for that place, but twice for others, till 1780. In 1755, he was appointed one of the lords of trade; which office he held, during every change of administration, till it was abolished in 1780.

His character appears to have been amiable and respectable. As an author he attained no small degree of reputation, by fine talents, which had every aid that useful and polite learning could bestow. He had a critical judgment, an elegant taste, and a rich vein of wit and humor. His "View of the Internal Evidences of the Christian Religion," abounds with just and important observations. It was written under a full conviction of the truth of the Christian dispensation, and from a sincere zeal for its service.

On his death-bed, it is said that, in looking over

his life, he particularly rejoiced in the belief, that his "View of the Internal Evidences" had been useful. He spoke of his death in such a manner as showed he was prepared to die. A very honorable testimony to his talents and merit was inscribed in the register of Bottisham, by William Lord Mansell, his parish minister. "He regrets the loss of one of the most amiable of men, and one of the truest Christians;—a man who possessed the finest understanding united to the best heart."

The following sentiments of Soame Jenyns, on the excellence of the spirit and precepts of the gospel, appear to have been formed so much under the influence of true religion, and contain so strong a testimony in favor of its divine efficacy, that they claim a place in this collection :

"Let us examine," says he, "what are the new precepts in the Christian religion, which peculiarly correspond with its object, the preparing us for the kingdom of heaven. Of these, the chief are, poorness of spirit, forgiveness of injuries, and charity to all men : to these, we may add repentance, faith, self-abasement, and a detachment from the world; all moral duties peculiar to this religion, and absolutely necessary to the attainment of its end.

"'Blessed are the poor in spirit; for theirs is the kingdom of heaven.' By which poorness of spirit is to be understood, a disposition of mind, meek, humble, submissive to power, void of ambition, patient of injuries, and free from all resentment. This was so new, and so opposite to the ideas of all Pagan moralists, that they thought this temper of mind a criminal and contemptible meanness, which must induce men to sacrifice the glory of their country, and their own honor, to a shameful pusillanimity : and such it appears to almost all who are called Christians, even at this day ; who not only reject it in practice, but disavow it in principle, notwithstanding this explicit declaration of their Master. We see them revenging the smallest affronts by premeditated murder, as individuals, on principles of honor ; and, in their national capacities, destroying each other with fire and sword, for the low considerations of commercial interests, the balance of rival powers, or the ambition of princes. we see them, with their last breath, animating each other to a savage revenge ; and, in the agonies of death, plunging, with feeble arms, their daggers into the hearts of their opponents : and, what is still worse, we hear all these barbarisms celebrated by historians ; flattered by poets ; applauded in theatres ; approved in senates ! and even sanctified in pulpits !

"But universal practice cannot alter the nature of things, nor universal error change the nature of truth. Pride was not made for man ; but humility, meekness, and resignation, that is, poorness of spirit, was made for man, and properly belongs to his dependent and precarious situation ; and is the only disposition of mind which can enable him to enjoy ease and quiet here, and happiness hereafter. Yet was this important precept entirely unknown, until it was promulgated by him who said : 'Suffer little children to come unto me, and forbid them not ; for of such is the kingdom of heaven : verily I say unto you, whosoever shall not receive the kingdom of God as a little child, shall in no wise enter therein.'

"Another precept, equally new, and no less excellent, is, forgiveness of injuries. 'Ye have heard,' says Christ to his disciples, 'Thou shalt love thy neighbor, and hate thine enemy : but I say unto you, love your enemies ; bless them that curse you ; do good to them that hate you ; and pray for them which despitefully use you, and persecute you.' This was a lesson, so new, and so utterly unknown, till taught by his doctrines, and enforced by his example, that the wisest moralists of the wisest nations and ages, represented the desire of revenge as a mark of a noble mind, and the accomplishment of it as one of the chief felicities attendant on a fortunate man. But how much more magnanimous, how much more beneficial to mankind, is forgiveness! It is more magnanimous, because every generous and exalted disposition of the human mind is requisite to the practice of it ; for these alone can enable us to bear the wrongs and insults of wickedness and folly with patience, and to look down on the perpretrators of them, with pity rather than indignation : these alone can teach us, that such are but a part of those sufferings allotted to us in this state of probation ; and to know that to overcome evil with good, is the most glorious of all victories. It is the most beneficial, because this amiable conduct alone can put an end to a continual succession of injuries and retaliations ; for every retaliation becomes a new injury, and requires another act of revenge for satisfaction.

"But would we observe this salutary precept, to love our enemies, and to do good to those who despitefully use us, this obstinate benevolence would at last conquer the most inveterate hearts, and we should have no enemies to forgive. How much more exalted a character, therefore, is a Christian martyr, suffering with resignation, and praying for the guilty, than a Pagan hero, breathing revenge, and destroying the innocent! Yet, noble and useful as this virtue is, before the appearance of this religion, it was not only unpractised, but decried in principle, as mean and ignominious, though so obvious a remedy for most of the miseries of this life; and so necessary a qualification for the happiness of the next.

"Repentance is another new moral duty strenuously insisted on by this religion. But no repentance can remove our depravity, unless it be such as entirely changes the nature and disposition of the offender ; which, in the language of Scripture, is called 'being born again.' Mere contrition for past crimes, and even the pardon of them, cannot effect this, unless it operate to this entire conversion, or new birth, as it is properly and emphatically named; for sorrow can no more purify a mind corrupted by a long continuance in vicious habits, than it can restore health to a body distempered by a long course of vice and intemperance.

"Hence, also, every one who is in the least acquainted with himself, may judge of the reasonableness of the hope that is in him, and of his situation in a future state, by his present condition. If he feels in himself a temper proud, turbulent, vindictive, and malevolent, and a violent attachment to the pleasures or business of the world, he may be assured that he must be excluded from the kingdom of heaven; not only because his conduct can attract no such reward; but because, if admitted, he would find there no objects satisfactory to his passions, inclinations, and pursuits.

"Faith is another moral duty enjoined by this institution, and recommended in the New Testament; where, in general, it signifies an humble, teachable, and candid disposition, a trust in God, and confidence in his declarations and promises; and it is always a direct contrast to pride, obstinacy, and self-conceit.

"Self-abasement is another moral duty inculcated by this religion only; which requires us to impute even our own virtues to the grace and favor of our Creator; and to acknowledge that we can do nothing good by our own powers, unless assisted by his over-ruling influence. This doctrine seems, at first sight, to infringe on our free-will, and to deprive us of all merit; but, on a closer examination, the truth of it may be demonstrated both by reason and experience: it is evident that, in fact, it does not impair the one, or depreciate the other; and that it is productive of so much humility, resignation, and dependence on God, that it justly claims a place amongst the most illustrious moral virtues.

"Detachment from the world is another moral virtue constituted by this religion alone; so new that, even at this day, few of its professors can be persuaded that it is required, or that it is any virtue at all. By this detachment from the world, is not to be understood a seclusion from society, abstraction from all business, or retirement to a gloomy cloister. Industry and labor, cheerfulness and hospitality, are frequently recommended; nor is the acquisition of wealth and honors prohibited, if they can be obtained by honest means, and a moderate degree of attention and care: but such an unremitted anxiety, and perpetual application, as engross our whole time and thoughts, are forbidden; because they are incompatible with the spirit of this religion, and most utterly disqualify us for the attainment of its great end. We toil on in the vain pursuits and frivolous occupations of the world, die in our harness, and then expect, if no gigantic crime stand in the way, to step immediately into the kingdom of heaven : but without a previous detachment from the business of this world, we cannot be prepared for the happiness of another.

" Yet this could make no part of the morality of Pagans, because their virtues were altogether connected with this business, and consisted chiefly in conducting it with honor to themselves, and benefit to the public. Christianity has a nobler object in view, which, if not attended to, must be lost for ever. This object is that celestial mansion, of which we should never lose sight, and to which we should be ever advancing, during our journey through life: but this by no means precludes us from performing the business, or enjoying the amusements, of travellers, provided they detain us not too long, nor lead us out of our way.

" Another precept, first noticed and first enjoined by this institution, is, charity to all men. What this is, we may best learn from the admirable description, contained in the following words: ' Charity suffereth long, and is kind; charity envieth not, charity vaunteth not itself; is not puffed up; doth not behave itself unseemly; seeketh not her own; is not easily provoked; thinketh no evil; rejoiceth not in iniquity, but rejoiceth in the truth; beareth all things; believeth all things; hopeth all things; endureth all things.'

" Here we have an accurate delineation of this bright constellation of all virtues; which consists not, as many imagine, in the building of monasteries, endowment of hospitals, or the distribution of alms; but in such an amiable disposition of mind, as exercises itself every hour in acts of kindness, patience, complacence, and benevolence to all around us; and which alone is able to promote happiness in the present life, or render us capable of receiving it in another.

"And yet this is totally new, and so it is declared to be, by the Author of it: 'A new commandment I give unto you, that ye love one another; as I have loved you, that ye love one another; by this shall all men know that ye are my disciples, if ye have love one to another.' This benevolent disposition is made the great characteristic of a Christian, the test of his obedience, and the mark by which he is to be distinguished.

"This love for each other, is that charity just now described, and contains all those qualities which are there attributed to it; humility, patience, meekness, and beneficence: without which we must live in perpetual discord, and consequently cannot pay obedience to this commandment of loving one another: a commandment so sublime, so rational, and so beneficial, so wisely calculated to correct the depravity, diminish the wickedness, and abate the miseries of human nature, that, did we universally comply with it, we should soon be relieved from all the inquietudes arising from our own unruly passions, anger, envy, revenge, malice, and ambition;

as well as from all those injuries, to which we are perpetually exposed, from the indulgence of the same passions in others. It would also preserve our minds in such a state of tranquility, and so prepare them for the kingdom of heaven, that we should slide out of a life of peace, love, and benevolence, into that celestial society, by an almost imperceptible transition."

SECTION III.

LORD LYTTELTON.

GEORGE LYTTELTON, the son of Sir Thomas Lyttelton, of Hagley, in Worcestershire, was born in 1709. He was educated at Eton, and was so much distinguished there, that his exercises were recommended as models to his schoolfellows. At the university of Oxford, where his education was completed, he pursued his classical studies with uncommon avidity and success; and retained the same reputation of superiority.

As a writer, both in prose and verse, Lord Lyttelton attained considerable eminence; and, by his great abilities and integrity, became highly useful to his country.

In the pride of juvenile confidence, with the help of corrupt conversation, he had entertained doubts of the truth of Christianity; but, about the thirty-eighth year of his age, he thought the time come when it was no longer fit to doubt or believe by chance, and applied himself seriously to the great question. His studies, being honest, ended in conviction. He found that religion was true, and what he had learned he endeavored to teach, by "Observations on the Conversion of St. Paul;" a treatise to which infidelity has never been able to fabricate a specious answer. This book, his father had the happiness of seeing, and expressed his pleasure in a letter which deserves to be inserted:

"I have read your religious treatise with infinite pleasure and satisfaction. The style is fine and clear, the arguments close, cogent, and irresistible. May the King of kings, whose glorious cause you have so well defended, reward your pious labors; and grant that I may be found worthy, through the merits of Jesus Christ, to be an eye-witness of that happiness, which I do not doubt he will bountifully bestow upon you! In the meantime, I shall never cease glorifying God, for having endowed you with such useful talents, and given me so good a son.

"Your affectionate father,
"Thomas Lyttelton."

After a life spent in honorable pursuits, this distinguished person was seized with a severe illness, about the sixty-fourth year of his age, which soon proved mortal. Of his death, a very affecting and instructive account has been given by his physician.

" On Sunday evening, the symptoms of his lordship's disorder, which for a week past had alarmed us, put on a fatal appearance; and his lordship believed himself to be a dying man. From this time he suffered by restlessness, rather than pain.

Though his nerves were apparently much fluttered, his mental faculties never seemed stronger, when he was thoroughly awake.

"Though his lordship wished his approaching dissolution not to be lingering, he waited for it with resignation. He said, 'It is a folly, a keeping me in misery, now to attempt to prolong life :' yet he was easily persuaded, for the satisfaction of others, to do or take any thing thought proper for him. On Saturday, he had been remarkably better, and we were not without some hopes of his recovery.

"On Sunday, about eleven in the forenoon, his lordship sent for me : he said he felt a great hurry of spirits, and wished to have a little conversation with me, in order to divert it. He then proceeded to open the fountain of that heart, from whence goodness had so long flowed, as from a copious spring. 'When I first set out in the world,' said he, 'I had friends who endeavored to shake my belief in the Christian religion. I saw difficulties which staggered me ; but I kept my mind open to conviction. The evidences and doctrines of Christianity, studied with attention, made me a most firm and persuaded believer of the Christian religion. I have made it the rule of my life, and it is the ground of my future hopes. I have erred and sinned ; but have repented, and never indulged any vicious habit. In politics, and public life, I have made public good the rule of my conduct. I never gave counsels which I did not at the time think best. I have seen that I was sometimes in the wrong; but I did not err designedly. I have endeavored, in private life, to do all the good in my power; and never for a moment could indulge malicious or unjust designs upon any person whatsoever.'

"At another time he said: 'I must leave my soul in the same state it was in before my illness; I find this a very inconvenient time for solicitude about any thing.'

"On the evening, when the symptoms of death came on, he said: 'I shall die; but it will not be your fault.' When Lord and Lady Valentia came to see his lordship, he gave them his solemn benediction, and said: 'Be good, be virtuous, my lord; you must come to this.' Thus he continued giving his dying benediction to all around him. On Monday morning, a lucid interval gave some small hopes, but these vanished in the evening; and he continued dying, though with very little uneasiness, till Tuesday morning, August 22, (1773,) when, between seven and eight o'clock, he expired almost without a groan."

12*

SECTION IV.

JONAS HANWAY.

A PERSON so disinterested in private life, and so religiously concerned for the happiness of others, as was the distinguished Jonas Hanway, demands a place in these memoirs. This excellent man devoted his time, his fortune, his powers of body and mind, to the service of his fellow-creatures. To improve the morals of the poor, to alleviate their distresses, and to provide for their offspring suitable instruction and useful employment, were objects he had much at heart; and a great part of his life was spent in promoting these benevolent views. It may justly be said of him, that, next to his reverence for the Divine Being, the love of human kind was the strongest feeling of his breast; and that, when he had engaged in any office of general benevolence, no obstacles, but those which were insuperable, could discourage his active perseverance.

As he well knew how much the happiness of the poorer classes of mankind depends on frugality and habitual industry, he studied to promote amongst them virtues so necessary to their condition. It gave him a very sensible pleasure, when any of the numerous objects of his charity, who came to pay him their respects, were cleanly and neatly dressed, and appeared with cheerful and contented countenances. He treated them with respect and attention; entered into their concerns with paternal affection; and let them know that, on any real emergency, they might with confidence apply to him. It was this, rather than the largeness of his gifts, that endeared him so much to the people. He never walked out, but he was followed by the good wishes, silent or expressed, of some to whom he had afforded relief. To meet the grateful eyes of persons whom he had served, was to him a high enjoyment; and no one partook of it oftener.

This benevolent and pious man, through the whole course of his life, remembered that he was an accountable being. He examined his own conduct, with the same degree of severity which men too often adopt in their scrutiny into the conduct of others; and considered that the time would come, and might not be far off, when he should reflect with sorrow on every bad action. There are many well-disposed men, who, knowing that death is inevitable, endeavor to banish from their minds the awful thought; but Hanway seemed to derive a solemn pleasure from indulging the idea. To excite the frequent recollection of his condition and end, he caused to be inscribed on a plate of brass the following lines, which seemed to have

been designed as his epitaph, and which he often
seriously reviewed :

> " I believe that my Redeemer liveth,
> And that I shall also rise from
> The grave,
> JONAS HANWAY ;
> Who, trusting in that good Providence
> Which so visibly governs the world,
> Passed through a variety of fortunes with
> Patience ;
>
> Living the greater part of his days
> In foreign lands, ruled by arbitrary power,
> He received the deeper impression
> Of the happy constitution of his own country ;
> Whilst
> The persuasive laws contained in the
> New Testament,
> And the consciousness of his own depravity,
> Softened his heart to a sense
> Of the various wants of his
> Fellow-creatures.
>
> Reader,
> Inquire no further :
> The Lord have mercy on his soul and thine !

" Apprehensive of the too partial regard of his friends, and
esteeming plain truth above the proudest trophies of monu-
mental flattery; at the age of fifty-one, he caused this plate
and inscription to be made."

In the summer of 1786, his health sensibly declined ; and he perceived that he was verging towards that state, which he had often contemplated
with solemn complacence. During the progress of
a tedious, and sometimes very painful illness, he
never expressed the least impatience. When he

grew so weak as to be confined to his bed, he requested his physicians to speak frankly, and without reserve, of his disorder: and when he was convinced that he could not recover, he sent and paid all his tradesmen; he took leave of his most intimate friends; dictated some letters to absent acquaintances; and discoursed concerning his affairs with tranquillity, and even with cheerfulness. To his surgeon, who attended him with unceasing anxiety, he said: "If you think it will be of service in your practice, or to any one who may come after me, I beg you will have my body opened: I am willing to do as much good as possible."

He expressed his satisfaction, that his mind had never wandered or been perplexed, in any part of his illness. In the morning previous to his death he said to an intimate friend: "I have no uncomfortable reflections concerning my approaching end; but I find life so strong, that I think I shall not leave the world without a sharp conflict." Soon after this the disorder increased, and put a period to a long and valuable life, spent in promoting the glory of God, and the good of mankind.

The following stanzas are worthy of a place in the character of this truly pious and benevolent man:

And thou, blest Hanway! long thy country's prayer,
  Exulting now in kindred worlds above,
Co-heir of Howard! deign the muse to hear,
  Though angels greet thee with a brother's love.

Far though removed from this diminished earth,
  A crown of glory beaming on thy brow,
The God who fixed it there—to note thy worth,
  Bids the rapt lyre with all thy spirit glow.

Warm in the way, behold what myriads come,
  While tears of ecstasy and anguish flow!
Their blended incense pouring on thy tomb,
  To mark an empire's joy, an empire's wo.

Close to thy Howard—O congenial shade!
  On the pure column shall thy bust have place;
Though deep in every bosom is portrayed
  Those grateful records time shall ne'er erase.

The generous plan that public virtue draws,
  The fair design that charity imparts,
The genius kindling in Religion's cause,
  Cherish their champion in our faithful hearts.

Near Hanway's bust the Magdalen shall kneel,
  A chasten'd votary of Compassion's dome;*
With pious awe the holiest ardors feel,
  And bless the founder of her peaceful home:

And O, Philanthropy! thy heav'n-rear'd fane†
  Shall oft avow the good man's zeal divine,
When bounty leads a poor and orphan train
  To clasp their little arms round Hanway's shrine.

Transcendent energies of grace sublime,
  Whose magic goodness work'd with double power
Cradled the outcast babe who knew no crime,
  And bade the sinner turn and blush no more.

Ah, full of honors as of years, farewell!
  Thus o'er thy ashes shall Britannia sigh;
Each age, each sex, thy excellence shall tell,
  Which taught the young to live, the old to die!

* The Magdalen House.   † The Foundling Hospital.

SECTION V.

ANTHONY BENEZET.

Anthony Benezet was born in France, in the year 1713. The persecution on account of religious opinions, which then existed in that country, induced his parents to leave France. After a residence of many years in London, they and their son, the subject of this memoir, went to America, and settled in Philadelphia.

He was a man of sound understanding, of great piety, humility, and self-denial, and of a very benevolent disposition. Being desirous of spending his life in a manner the most useful to his fellow-creatures, he devoted himself to the education of youth. In this arduous, but truly honorable employment, he passed about forty years; and acquitted himself very much to the satisfaction of parents and children. His great object was, to imbue the minds of his pupils with reverence for religion, and to train them up in a course of virtue. Pecuniary advantages were of small moment in his estimation, of which he gave many striking proofs.

A short time before his decease, he declared, in a letter to a friend, that though leisure and retirement would be very agreeable to him, he was well satisfied to remain in his occupation; and that he knew no other, whatever might be its advantages, for which he would exchange his employment, unless it were a commission to preach and propagate, as a minister, the Gospel of Christ.

When the .school established in Philadelphia, "for the instruction of black people and their offspring," was suspended, on account of the indisposition of their teacher, he voluntarily surrendered his own school to other competent persons, and undertook the education of those people, though, in a pecuniary respect, he lost considerably by the change. His humility, and his sympathy with that unhappy race of men, disposed him to think no condescensions degrading, by which he could be peculiarly useful to them: and he was greatly desirous, that they might be so improved in their minds, as to render the freedom which they had lately recovered, a real blessing to themselves, and a benefit to the State.

He was a friend to the poor and distressed of every description, and labored most earnestly for their relief and welfare. It may indeed be said of him, that his whole life was spent in going about doing good to men. He appeared to do every thing, as if the words of his Saviour were continually sounding in his ears: "Wist ye not that I must be about my Father's business?" He was, as Dr. Rush observed, a man of truly catholic spirit; one who loved piety and virtue in others, wherever he found them; and who respected all sincere worshippers of God, in whatever manner that worship was performed.

The miseries of the enslaved Africans, and the great injustice done to them, very deeply affected his compassionate heart. He published many tracts on the subject; supported an extensive correspondence with persons in Europe and America, who were likely to aid his benevolent views; and exerted himself to the utmost, to ameliorate the condition of the negroes, and to procure the entire abolition of the trade. As he was one of the earliest advocates of these injured men, and indefatigably pursued his object, we may fairly attribute to his labors, with the Divine blessing upon them, a great part of that spirit of inquiry into their situation, and sympathy with their distresses, which have spread over the world; and which, we trust, will, ere long, destroy this system of inhumanity and injustice.

About a year before his decease, his health became much impaired; but being of a lively disposition, very temperate, and zealously concerned to occupy his talents to the last, he supported his school, till he was quite disabled from performing the duties of it. But his charity and beneficence continued with life. The last time he walked across his room, was to take from his desk six dollars, which he gave to a poor widow whom he

had long assisted to maintain. Three hours before
his death, he delivered to his executors a number
of tracts, in sheets, on religious subjects, with directions for their being bound and dispersed. He
devised nearly the whole of his estate, after the
decease of his wife, to trustees, for the support and
benefit of the Negro school, of which he had been
the tutor. And thus, having lived a most useful
and exemplary life, he was well prepared for the
approach of death. He endured his pains with
much patience; and, with Christian composure of
mind, resigned this mortal life, in the firm expectation of a happy immortality.

The loss of this beneficent man was deeply felt
by his fellow-citizens; and his funeral was attended
by a great number of persons of all ranks, and of
all religious professions; and many hundreds of
Negroes joined the procession. It may justly be
said, that, "the mourners went about the streets,"
and that his death was embalmed with tears. An
officer, who had served in the American army during the late war, in returning from the funeral,
pronounced a striking eulogium upon him. It contained but a few words: "I would rather," said
he, "be Anthony Benezet, in that coffin, than
George Washington, with all his fame."

SECTION VI.

AMES HERVEY.

JAMES HERVEY, an ingenious and pious clergyman, and a very popular writer, was born at Hard-
ingstone, in Northamptonshire, in the year 1714.
He had his education at the free grammar school
at Northampton ; and at Lincoln college, in Oxford. After a residence of seven years, he left the
university; and became, in 1736, curate to his
father, then possessed of the living of Weston-
Favell. He was an excellent scholar, being master
of the three learned languages, and well-read in
the classics.

In 1750, at his father's death, he succeeded to
the livings of Weston and Collingtree; which
being within five miles of each other, he attended
alternately with his curate, till the ill state of his
health confined him to Weston. Here he afterwards constantly resided, and diligently pursued
his labors, both in his ministerial office, and in his
study, as long as possible, under the disadvantage
of a weak constitution. He did not satisfy himself
with preaching only on the Lord's day ; but, whilst
his strength permitted him, held a regular lecture

in the middle of the week, which was very well attended. He also diligently catechised the children of his parishioners, and was regular in his pastoral visits at their houses, till he was confined to his own, when he encouraged them to come to him, for his friendly and religious advice. By these exertions, as well as the labors of his study, he fell into a decline, attended with an almost incessant hectic cough, and much acute pain, which he supported with most exemplary patience.

In 1746, he published his "Meditations among the Tombs," and "Reflections on a Flower Garden;" and the following year appeared the "Contemplations on the Night and Starry Heavens;" and "A Winter Piece." The sublime sentiments in these Pieces are conveyed in a flowing and elegant style. They have been much read; and are eminently calculated to cherish pious and grateful emotions towards the God of nature, and the Source of every blessing. In 1775, he published his "Theron and Aspasio, or a Series of Letters and Dialogues on the most Important Subjects." He was the author of several other works, which bear the marks of genius, and of a truly benevolent and religious mind.

His moral character was highly exemplary; his temper placid, disinterested, unaffectedly humble; and in his transactions with others, he was ever cheerful, punctual, just, and candid to persons of every denomination. He sometimes met with very cross occurrences; but he ever rose above them; he was never known to be in a passion. His humility rendered him invulnerable. When he was misrepresented and calumniated, he used to say: "Our enemies are sometimes our best friends, and tell us useful truths; and then we should amend our faults, and be thankful for such information. If what they say be not true, and spoken from malice only, then such persons are to be considered as diseased in their minds, and ought to be prayed for. They are to be pitied; and I might as justly be angry with men who are diseased in their bodies." All this he spoke with humility, seriousness, and great sweetness of spirit: for it was the language of his heart, and not of affectation.

In actions of benevolence and charity, though he had some equals, it is certain that he had no superiors, as far as his means extended. He preferred clothing the poor, and supplying them with necessary articles, on the best terms, to giving them money. "I am," said he, "God's steward for the poor; and I must husband the little pittance I have to bestow upon them, and make it go as far as possible." But, on special occasions, when money would be particularly useful, he would give to a prudent housekeeper, distressed by sickness or misfortunes, five or more guineas at a time; and he was, on all proper occasions, careful that it should not be known from whom the money came.

By his last will, he bequeathed the future profits

of all his works to benevolent uses; excepting his "Meditations," the copy of which he sold during his lifetime, and applied the sums arising from its sale and former impressions, amounting to about seven hundred pounds, to the relief of the poor and distressed. He said that this money was devoted to God; and that he would on no account apply it to worldly uses; that he wrote, not for profit or fame, but to serve the cause of religion: and as Providence had blessed his attempts, he thought himself bound to relieve the distresses of his fellow-creatures, with the product of his labors.

The cultivation of real religion and holiness in heart and life, which this good man strenuously recommended, induced some persons to charge him with holding tenets injurious to society, and calculated to make men melancholy, and regardless of the lawful concerns of this world. But every charge of this nature is abundantly refuted by his writings, and the whole tenor of his life; and particularly by an excellent and striking passage, in his "Contemplations on the Starry Heavens;" from which the following lines are extracted:

"Some, I believe, are apt to imagine, that they must abandon all the satisfactions of *this* world, if they become zealous candidates for the felicity of *another*. But this is a very mistaken notion. Religion was never intended to strike off the wheels of business, or to cut asunder the sinews of industry; but rather, to make men industrious from a principle of conscience, not from the instigations of avarice; that so they may promote their immortal happiness, even while they provide for their temporal maintenance. It has no design to extirpate our passions, but only to restrain their irregularities: neither would it extinguish the delights of sense, but prevent them from evaporating into vanity, and subsiding into gall. A person may be cheerful among his friends, and yet joyful in God. He may taste the sweets of this earthly estate; and, at the same time, cherish his hopes of a nobler inheritance in heaven."

Though this sincere Christian was ardent and laborious, in serving his Great Master, and in promoting the religious welfare of his fellow-creatures; yet he had a very humble sense of his own services; and expressed to his friends, during his indisposition, great regret that he had not embraced every opportunity afforded him, to advance the cause of his Redeemer. These expressions were made with much tenderness of spirit, and were accompanied with tears. But lest his sentiments and views should be misinterpreted, he added: " Do not think that I am afraid to die. I assure you I am not. I know what my Saviour hath done for me, and I long to be dismissed. But I wonder at the love of Christ, in doing so much for me; and lament to think how little I have done for him."

On a particular occasion, when his physician was

taking his leave, he observed to him, with great affection and sensibility, that as he had, not long before, a dangerous fall from his horse, by which he was much bruised; and as he had been lately ill, and then looked very pale; he hoped he would reflect on those narrow escapes, so often fatal to others, as a kind of warning from God to him, and remember them as such; adding: "How careful ought we to be, to improve those years which remain, at a time of life when but few can remain FOR US!"

The last illness of this truly excellent man commenced in the autumn of the year 1758; and, in a few months, made a great and affecting progress. His strength became exhausted, his body extremely emaciated, and his whole frame so sore, that he could scarcely bear to be touched, when it was necessary to move him. Yet, under all this calamity, he was ever praising God for his mercies, and for enduing him with patience.

About three hours before his death, he strongly and affectionately urged a friend of his who was present, to pay all due attention to the care of his everlasting concerns, as here there is no abiding-place, no continuing city. He entreated him not to be overcharged with the cares of this life; but to attend, amidst the multiplicity of his business, to the "one thing needful."

The physician observing the great difficulty and pain with which he spoke, (for he was almost suffocated with phlegm and frequent vomitings,) and perceiving by his pulse, that the pangs of death were coming on, desired that he would spare himself.

"No," said he, "doctor, no. You tell me I have but a few moments to live: oh! let me spend them in adoring our great Redeemer." He then repeated the 26th verse of the 73d Psalm: "Though my flesh and my heart fail me, yet God is the strength of my heart, and my portion for ever:" and he expatiated in a most striking manner, on these words of the Apostle: "All things are yours, life and death; for ye are Christ's." "Here," said he, "is the treasure of a Christian. Death is reckoned in this inventory; and a noble treasure it is. How thankful am I for death, as it is the passage through which I go to the Lord and Giver of eternal life; and as it frees me from all the misery you now see me endure, and which I am willing to endure, as long as God thinks fit: for I know he will, by and by, in his own good time, dismiss me from the body. These light afflictions are but for a moment, and then comes an eternal weight of glory. O! welcome, welcome death! Thou mayest well be reckoned among the treasures of the Christian. To live is Christ, but to die is gain."

After these expressions, as the doctor was taking his final leave of him, the dying saint expressed great gratitude for his visits and attentions, though it had been long out of the power of medicines to

cure him. He then paused a little; and being
raised in his chair, he, with great serenity and
sweetness of countenance, though the pangs of
death were upon him, repeated these words:
"Lord, now lettest thou thy servant depart in
peace, according to thy most holy and comfortable
word, for mine eyes have seen thy salvation."

In about an hour after he had uttered these expressions, he yielded up his pious soul to God, without a sigh or struggle, in the forty-fifth year of his
age.

SECTION VII.

ALTAMONT;

OR. THE DEATH OF THE LIBERTINE.

THE following account of an affecting, mournful exit, and the reflections that accompany it, are solemn and impressive. We shall present them to the reader, in the words of Doctor Young, who was present at the melancholy scene :

"Is not the death-bed of a profligate a prime school of wisdom? Are we not obliged, when we are invited to it? for what else should reclaim us? The pulpit? We are prejudiced against it. Besides, an agonizing profligate, though silent, outpreaches the most celebrated the pulpit ever knew. But, if he speaks, his words might instruct the best instructors of mankind. Mixed in the warm converse of life, we think with men; on a death-bed, with God.

"There are two lessons of this school written, as it were, in capitals, which they who run may read. First, he that, in this his minority, this field of discipline and conflict, instead of grasping the weapons of his warfare, is for ever gathering flowers, and catching at butterflies, with his unarmed hand, ever making idle pleasure his pursuit, must pay for it his vast reversion : and on opening his final account, (of which a death-bed breaks the seal,) shall find himself a beggar, a beggar past beggary; and shall passionately wish that his very being were added to the rest of his loss.

"Secondly, he shall find that truth, Divine truth, however, through life, injured, wounded, suppressed, is victorious, immortal : that, though with mountains overwhelmed, it will, one day, burst out like the fires of Etna; visible, bright, and tormenting, as the most raging flame. This now (oh, my friend!) I shall too plainly prove.

"The sad evening before the death of the noble youth, whose last hours suggested these thoughts, I was with him. No one was present but his physician, and an intimate whom he loved, and whom he had ruined. At my coming in, he said : 'You and the physician are come too late. I have neither life nor hope. You both aim at miracles. You would raise the dead!' 'Heaven,' I said, 'was merciful—' 'Or,' exclaimed he, 'I could not have been thus guilty. What has it not done to bless, and to save me! I have been too strong for Omnipotence! I have plucked down ruin.' I said, 'The blessed Redeemer,—' 'Hold! hold! you wound me! That is the rock on which I split: I denied his name!'

"Refusing to hear any thing from me, or take

any thing from the physician, he lay silent, as far
as sudden darts of pain would permit, till the clock
struck: then with vehemence he exclaimed: 'Oh!
time! time! it is fit thou shouldst thus strike thy
murderer to the heart! How art thou fled for
ever! A month!—O, for a single week! I ask
not for years; though an age were too little for
the much I have to do.' On my saying, we could
not do too much, that heaven was a blessed place—
'So much the worse.—'Tis lost! 'tis lost! Heaven
is to me the severest place of hell!'

"Soon after, I proposed prayer: 'Pray you that
can. I never prayed. I cannot pray, nor need I.
Is not heaven on my side already? It closes with
my conscience. Its severest strokes but second my
own.' Observing that his friend was much touched
at this, even to tears, (who could forbear? I could
not,) with a most affectionate look, he said, 'Keep
those tears for thyself. I have undone thee: Dost
thou weep for me? That is cruel. What can pain
me more?'

"Here his friend, too much affected, would have
left him. 'No, stay—thou still mayest hope;
therefore hear me. How madly have I talked!
How madly hast thou listened, and believed! but
look on my present state, as a full answer to thee,
and to myself. This body is all weakness and pain;
but my soul, as if stung up by torment to greater
strength and spirit, is full powerful to reason; full
mighty to suffer. And that which thus triumphs

within the jaws of immortality, is doubtless, immortal. And, as for a Deity, nothing less than an Almighty could inflict what I feel.'

"I was about to congratulate this passive involuntary confessor, on his asserting the two prime articles of his creed, extorted by the rack of nature, when he thus very passionately exclaimed: 'No, no! let me speak on. I have not long to speak. My much injured friend! my soul, as my body, lies in ruins; in scattered fragments of broken thought! Remorse for the past, throws my thought on the future. Worse dread of the future, strikes it back on the past. I turn, and turn, and find no ray. Didst thou feel half the mountain that is on me, thou wouldst struggle with the martyr for his stake; and bless Heaven for the flames; that is not an everlasting flame; that is not an unquenchable fire.'

"How were we struck! yet, soon after, still more. With what an eye of distraction, what a face of despair, he cried out: 'My principles have poisoned my friend! my extravagance has beggared my boy! my unkindness has murdered my wife! And is there another hell? Oh! thou blasphemed, yet indulgent LORD GOD! hell itself is a refuge, if it hide me from thy frown!' Soon after his understanding failed. His terrified imagination uttered horrors not to be repeated, or ever forgotten. And ere the sun (which, I hope, has seen few like him) arose, the gay, young, noble, ingenuous, accomplished, and most wretched Altamont expired!

"If this is a man of pleasure, what is a man of pain? How quick, how total, is the transit of such persons! In what a dismal gloom they set for ever! How short, alas! the day of their rejoicing! For a moment they glitter, they dazzle! In a moment, where are they? Oblivion covers their memories! Ah! would it did! Infamy snatches them from oblivion. In the long-living annals of infamy their triumphs are recorded. Thy sufferings, poor Altamont! still bleed in the bosom of the heart-stricken friend—for Altamont had a friend. He might have had many. His transient morning might have been the dawn of an immortal day. His name might have been gloriously enrolled in the records of eternity. His memory might have left a sweet fragrance behind it, grateful to the surviving friend, salutary to the succeeding generation. With what capacity was he endowed! with what advantages for being greatly good! But with the talents of an angel, a man may be a fool. If he judges amiss in the supreme point, judging right in all else, but aggravates his folly: as it shows him wrong, though blessed with the best capacity of being right."

CHAPTER X.

SECTION I.

BARON HALLER.

Albert Haller, one of the most illustrious literary characters of his age, was the son of a citizen and advocate of Berne, where he was born, in the year 1708. The accounts of his early display of talents, are as extraordinary as almost any upon record. He chose the medical profession, in which he became very eminent. He was an anatomist, a physiologist, and a botanist, of the first order. It is not too much to say of him, that he was one of the best informed men in Europe. He wrote and spoke, with equal facility, the German, French, and Latin languages; and read all the other tongues of civilized Europe, except the Sclavonic dialects. His acquaintance with books was so extensive, that it would be difficult to point out any of the least note, which he had not perused, and of which the contents did not dwell upon his memory. He was a poet, too, of distinguished merit. The critics of Germany reckon Haller among the first who gave sublimity, richness, and harmony to their poetical language; and who described nature in its true colors.

The talents and knowledge of Haller, his works in various departments of science and literature, and his unblemished integrity and virtue, rendered him, in the highest degree, respectable among the learned of Europe; and his friendship and correspondence were courted by the most celebrated men of his time. He was professor of medicine in the university of Gottingen. He filled successively the botanical, chemical, and anatomical chairs; and raised the reputation of the university to a very high pitch. There he resided near seventeen years; and then returned to Berne, his native place, where he was elected a member of the sovereign council; and enjoyed the first authority in the administration of public affairs, till the time of his death, which took place in the year 1777.

This great and good man, in the early part of his life, had doubts concerning the objects of the Christian faith. But these doubts were dispelled by a successful application to every branch of science, on the one hand; and by a candid exam ination of the sacred oracles, on the other. The first, by purging his soul, according to his own emphatic phrase, of arrogance and pride, filled it with true poverty of spirit. The second convinced him that the Divine revelation, conveyed in the Holy Scriptures, is a boon worthy of the merciful Author of our nature to give; and such as is fit for guilty mortals to receive, with humble gratitude and reverence.

There are hours of mental depression in human life, which can neither be prevented nor remedied, by the most prosperous worldly circumstances, or by the greatest skill of man. The healing art, which Haller applied with singular success to the diseases of the body, could not, as he experienced in his own case, reach that dissatisfaction with the present, and that apprehension of a future state, which so frequently disturb the breasts of mankind. But he found other aids, which proved a sovereign remedy to all his fears and depressions. The Divine laws were to him a delightful subject of attention, and a joyful object of hope. His confidence in the goodness of God, refreshed his mind; and so fortified it, that he contemplated, without dismay, the king of terrors.

The consolations which he felt himself, he was anxious to impart to others. In imitation of the Saviour of the world, he went about doing good to the souls and the bodies of men. He eagerly seized the numberless opportunities, which his profession as a physician gave him, of convincing those with whom he conversed, of the truth, and of converting them to the practice of the Christian religion. And this he did, not only by his instructions, but by his example. For he was charitable to the poor; he sympathized in the tenderest manner with the distressed; and was humane and just in all his dealings with the sons of men.

A thousand incidents, which passed unheeded by the vulgar eye, recalled to his mind the Deity. And when he recollected or heard that *great name*, he gave way, in whatever company or circumstances he happened to be placed, to some pious ejaculations, with his eyes and hands lifted up towards heaven.

While his feeling mind embraced in the bonds of love all his fellow-creatures, and interested him in their present and future concerns, there was one person, whom God and nature had recommended to his peculiar tenderness and care. He had a daughter, dear to him as his own soul. He knew the inquietudes, to which the common lot of humanity would subject her through life; and the fears that would alarm her tender breast at the approach of death, of which it was some consolation to him, that "he should not live to be the mournful witness." To her he addressed, at different times, but in a regular succession, a number of letters, on the truths of the Christian religion. They were afterwards, by his permission, published for the benefit of the world at large. The work possesses great merit; and is particularly proper for the perusal and study of young persons.

We shall conclude our account of Baron Haller, with an extract from the last letter contained in the publication just mentioned. It marks the writer's high sense of the importance of religion; his solicitude for his daughter's happiness; and his strong confidence in the future rewards of piety and virtue:

"Let us employ the time that is present: eternity will be our reward, if we make a good use of it. Let us always have before our eyes the nature and consequences of sin: let us remember that it will deprive us of the favor of God, and expose us to his displeasure. Reflect on the value of that life and immortality which Christ has brought to light by the gospel. The enjoyments of this present short life, which are indeed but puerile amusements, must disappear, when placed in competition with the greatness and durability of the glory which is to come.

"By the mercy of God, we are restored from the lowest state of abasement and dejection. We are animated with the most comfortable promises. We now walk with confidence in that road, which has been marked out for us with so much wisdom; and which so well corresponds with our new desires and abilities. We leave behind us those vices which tended to estrange us from God and happiness: before us is a benevolent Being, who offers to the victorious, incorruptible crowns, as the recompense of victory; which victory he also helps us to gain. We may now rest satisfied with respect to our future condition, without perplexing ourselves about the trials we shall have to undergo, and which are yet at a distance. Let us be careful to employ to advantage the present hour. The means of salvation, the sacred writings, the precepts of our Saviour, are in our hands. We insensibly draw near to the desired harbor; the approaches of dissolution become less formidable, the nearer we advance to the happy mansions of eternity, where error and vice will be disarmed, and have no more power over us.

"Receive, my daughter, these most important of all truths, from a father, who considers himself on the verge of life: they are the most precious marks of tenderness which he can give you. These instructions would have been less imperfect, if his capacity had been more extensive. They are, however, the result of his reflections, and of the researches which he has made after truth; they are also the effect of his internal conviction. Your father, who now addresses you, has had his doubts; he has sometimes been mistaken; and has wished, in those moments, that the consequences of sin were not so grievous. He has not been exempt from falling: but the victorious grace of God has kindly come to his relief.

"The king of terrors approaches me with hasty

steps: but I behold his advances without dismay. Beyond that era of my existence, I see objects of joy and hope, which invite me to leave this world, and to step forward into eternity; into mansions of holiness and bliss, where death shall be banished for ever, and where sin shall have no place. After having finished your course, you will, I trust, again meet your father, in those glorious and peaceful abodes, where the idea of our frail mortality shall no longer disturb our breasts, or fill them with shame; and where the miseries of this life shall no longer draw tears from our eyes."

SECTION II.

JOHN HOWARD.

JOHN HOWARD, the indefatigable friend of the poor and unfortunate, was born at Hackney, in the year 1726. Of his character and pious labors, Dr. Aikin speaks in the following terms:

"Among those truly illustrious persons who, in the several ages and nations of the world, have marked their track through life, by a continued course of doing good, few have been so distinguished either by the extent of the good produced, or by the purity of motive and energy of character exhibited in the process of doing it, as the late John Howard. To have adopted the cause of the prisoner, the sick, and the destitute, not only in his own country, but throughout Europe; to have considerably alleviated the burden of present misery among those unfortunate classes, and, at the same time, to have provided for the reformation of the vicious, and the prevention of future crimes and calamities; to have been instrumental in the actual establishment of many plans of humanity and utility, and to have laid the foundation for much more improvement hereafter; and to have done all this, as a private, unaided individual, struggling with toils, dangers, and difficulties, which might have appalled the most resolute; is surely a range of beneficence, which scarcely ever before came within the compass of one man's exertions."

Attachment to religion was a principle which had been imbibed by Howard in his youth; and which continued steady and uniform through life. Though he seems early to have made up his mind, as to the doctrines he thought best founded, and the mode of worship he most approved, yet religion abstractly considered, as the relation between man and his Maker, and the grand support of morality, appears to have been the principal object of his regard. This excellent principle enlarged his heart, and led him to commiserate the distresses of his fellow-creatures of every description; and at length prompted him to devote his life to the relief of suffering humanity.

Deeply impressed with a sense of the importance of his designs, and of the uncertainty of human life, he was desirous of doing as much as possible within the allotted limits. And the number of prisons and hospitals which he visited, in a short period of time, is surprising. The pious and well-governed disposition by which he was actuated, is forcibly expressed in the following passage extracted from one of his interesting publications:

"To my country I commit the result of my past labors. It is my intention again to quit it, for the purpose of revisiting Russia, Turkey, and some other countries, and extending my tour in the East. I am not insensible of the dangers that must attend such a journey. Trusting, however, in the protection of that kind Providence which has hitherto preserved me, I calmly and cheerfully commit myself to the disposal of unerring Wisdom. Should it please God to cut off my life in the prosecution of this design, let not my conduct be uncandidly imputed to rashness or enthusiasm: but to a serious, deliberate conviction, that I am pursuing the path of duty; and to a sincere desire of being made an instrument of greater usefulness to my fellow-creatures, than could be expected in the narrow circle of a retired life."

A little before the last time of his leaving England, when a friend expressed his concern at parting with him, from an apprehension that they should never meet again, he cheerfully replied: "We shall soon meet in heaven;" and, as he rather expected to die of the plague in Egypt, he added: "The way to heaven from Grand Cairo is as near as from London." He said he was perfectly easy as to the event; and made use of the words of Father Paul, who, when his physicians told him he had not long to live, said: "It is well: whatever pleases God, pleases me."

That in his singular and extensive course of beneficence he was not influenced by a desire of attracting the notice, or gaining the applause, of

his fellow-creatures, appears from his general life
and conduct; and is particularly evident, from the
spirit and firmness with which he opposed the
design, formed by many persons of distinction in
this country, to erect a statue, or some other
monument, to his honor.

The following passages are selected from some
of his letters on this subject: "To hasten to the
other very distressing affair; oh, why could not
my friends, who know how much I detest such
parade, have stopped so hasty a measure! As a
private man with some peculiarities, I wished to
retire into obscurity and silence. Indeed, my
friend, I cannot bear the thought of being thus
dragged out. I immediately wrote; and I hope
something may be done to stop it. My best
friends must disapprove the measure. It deranges
and confounds all my schemes; my exaltation is
my fall, my misfortune. My best and most intimate friends have, I see by the papers, been so
kind as not to subscribe to what you so justly term
a hasty measure. Indeed, if nothing now can be
done—I speak from my heart—never poor creature
was more dragged out in public."

That in all this there was no affectation, clearly
appeared from the letter he sent to the sub-
scribers; in which, after expressing his gratitude, he displayed so determined a repugnance
against admitting the proposed honor, deprecat-
ing it as the severest of punishments, that noth-

ing could be urged in reply, and the business was dropped.

Whilst this great and good man was ardently laboring for the relief of distress, it pleased Divine Providence to suffer him to fall a victim to a disease, supposed to be the plague, at Cherson, in the beginning of the year 1790. He was perfectly sensible, during his illness, except at short intervals, till within a very few hours before his death. He was fully prepared for the event, and often said, that he had no wish for life, but as it gave him the means of relieving his fellow-creatures.

A celebrated orator* has passed so fine a eulogium on the character of this excellent man, that we insert it with particular satisfaction :

" I cannot name this gentleman without remarking, that his labors and writings have done much to open the eyes and hearts of mankind. He has visited all Europe,—not to survey the sumptuousness of palaces, or the stateliness of temples ; not to make accurate measurements of the remains of ancient grandeur, nor to form a scale of the curiosity of modern art ; nor to collect medals, or collate manuscripts : but to dive into the depths of dungeons ; to plunge into the infection of hospitals ; to survey the mansions of sorrow and pain ; to take the guage and dimensions of misery, depression, and contempt ; to remember the forgotten, to attend to the neglected, to visit the for-

* Burke.

saken, and compare and collate the distresses of all men in all countries. His plan is original: it is as full of genius as it is of humanity. It was a voyage of discovery; a circumnavigation of charity. Already the benefit of his labor is felt more or less in every country. I hope he will anticipate his final reward, by seeing all its effects fully realized in his own."

We shall conclude the account of this benevolent man, with a few beautiful lines, written on his death, by Dr. Aikin:

> HOWARD, thy task is done! thy Master calls,
> And summons thee from Cherson's distant walls.
> "Come, well-approved! my faithful servant, come!
> No more a wand'rer, seek thy destined home.
> Long have I marked thee, with o'erruling eye,
> And sent admiring angels from on high,
> To walk the paths of danger by thy side,
> From death to shield thee, and through snares to guide.
> My minister of good, I've sped the way,
> And shot through dungeon glooms a leading ray,
> To cheer, by thee, with kind, unhop'd relief,
> My creatures, lost and 'whelmed in guilt and grief.
> I've led thee, ardent, on through wond'ring climes,
> To combat human woes and human crimes.
> But 'tis enough!—thy great commission's o'er;
> I prove thy faith, thy love, thy zeal, no more.
> Nor droop, that far from country, kindred, friends,
> Thy life, to duty long devoted, ends:
> What boots it *where* the high reward is giv'n,
> Or *whence* the soul, triumphant, springs to heav'n."

Dr. Aikin has written a judicious and interesting account of John Howard, under the title of " A View of the Character of John Howard, Esq.," to which we refer the reader for further information respecting this truly pious and worthy man.

SECTION III.

EWTON'S LETTERS.

THE following interesting examples of the power of religion on the minds of persons in humble life, are extracted from a work entitled " Cardiphonia, or the Utterance of the Heart :"*

"Though the grand evidence of those truths upon which our hopes are built, arises from the authority of God declaring them in his word, and revealing them by his Spirit to the awakened heart; (for till the heart is awakened, it is incapable of receiving this evidence;) yet some of these truths are so mysterious, so utterly repugnant to the judgment of depraved nature, that through the remaining influence of unbelief and vain reasoning, the temptations of Satan, and the subtle arguments with which some men, reputed wise, attack the foundations of our faith, the minds even of believers are sometimes capable of being shaken. I know no better corroborating evidence, for the relief of the mind under such assaults, than the testimony of dying persons ; especially of such

* By JOHN NEWTON, Rector of St. Mary, Woolnoth, London.

as have lived out of the noise of controversy, and who, perhaps, never heard a syllable of what has been started in these evil days, against some of the important articles of the Christian faith.

"Permit me, my lord, to relate, upon this occasion, some things which exceedingly struck me, in the conversation I had with a young woman, whom I visited in her last illness about two years ago. She was a sober, prudent person, of plain sense; she could read the Bible, but had read little besides. Her knowledge of the world was nearly confined to the parish; for I suppose she was seldom, if ever, twelve miles from home. She had known the Gospel about seven years before the Lord visited her with a lingering consumption, which, at length, removed her to a better world.

"A few days previous to her death, in prayer by her bedside, I thanked the Lord that he gave her now to see that she had not followed cunningly-devised fables. When I had finished, she repeated that expression: 'No,' said she, 'not cunningly-devised fables; these are realities indeed; I feel their truth; I feel their comfort. O, tell my friends, tell my acquaintance, tell inquiring souls, tell poor sinners, tell all the daughters of Jerusalem,' alluding to Solomon's Song, 'what Jesus has done for my soul! Tell them, that now, in the time of need, I find him my Beloved, and my Friend; and, as such, I commend him to them.'

"She then fixed her eyes steadfastly upon me

and proceeded, to the best of my recollection, as follows: 'Sir, you are highly favored, in being called to preach the gospel. I have often heard you with pleasure; but give me leave to tell you, that I now see all you have said, or that you can say, is comparatively but little. Nor till you come into my situation, and have death and eternity full in your view, will it be possible for you to conceive the vast weight and importance of the truths you declare. Oh! sir, it is a serious thing to die; no words can express what is needful to support the soul in the solemnity of a dying hour.'

"When I visited her again, she said: 'I feel that my hope is fixed upon the Rock of Ages: I know in whom I have believed. But the approach of death presents a prospect which is, till then, hidden from us, and which cannot be described.' She said much more to the same purpose: and in all she spoke, there were dignity, weight, and evidence. We may well say, with Elihu, 'Who teacheth like the Lord?'

"Many instances of the like kind I have met with here. I have a poor girl near me, whose natural capacity is very small; but the Lord has been pleased to make her acquainted alternately with great temptations, and proportionably great discoveries of his love and truth: sometimes, when her heart is enlarged, I listen to her with astonishment. I think no books or ministers I ever met with, have given me such an impression and understanding of what the Apostle styles, 'the deep things of God,' as I have, upon some occasions, received from her conversation.

"We have lost another of the people here: a person of much experience, eminent grace, wisdom, and usefulness. She walked with God forty years. She was one of the Lord's poor; but her poverty was decent, sanctified, and honorable. She lived respected, and her death is considered as a public loss. It is a great loss to me; I shall miss her advice and example, by which I have been often edified and animated. Almost the last words she uttered were: 'The Lord is my portion, saith my soul.'

"My attendance upon the sick is not always equally comfortable; but could I learn aright, it might be equally instructive. Some confirm to me the preciousness of a Saviour, by the cheerfulness with which, through faith in his name, they meet the king of terrors. Others no less confirm it, by the terror and reluctance they discover, when they find they must die. For though there are too many who sadly slight the blessed Gospel, while they are in health, yet, in this place, most are too far enlightened to be quite thoughtless about their souls, in their last illness, if they retain their senses. Then, like the foolish virgins, they say, 'Give us of your oil!'

"Through the Lord's goodness, several whom I have visited in these circumstances, have afforded me a comfortable hope. I have seen a marvellous and blessed change take place, in a few days, in their language, views, and temper. I now visit a young person, who is cut short in her nineteenth year, by a consumption, and who I think cannot live many days. I found her very ignorant and insensible, and she remained so a good while; but of late, I hope, her heart is touched. She feels her lost state; she seems to have some right desires; and I cannot but think the Lord is teaching her, and will reveal himself to her before she departs.

"But the scene is sometimes different. I saw a young woman die the last week. I had been often with her; but the night she was removed, she could only say, 'O, I cannot live! I cannot live!' She repeated this mournful complaint as long as she could speak: for, as the vital powers were more oppressed, her voice changed into groans; her groans grew fainter and fainter; and in about a quarter of an hour after she had done speaking, she expired. Poor creature! said I to myself, as I stood by her bedside, if you were a dutchess, in this situation, what could the world do for you now? I thought, likewise, how many things are there that now give us pleasure or pain, and assume a mighty importance in our view, which, in a dying hour, will be no more to us, than the clouds that fly unnoticed over our heads! Then the truth of our Lord's declaration will be seen and felt, and acknowledged: 'One thing is needful.' And we shall be ready to apply Grotius's dying confession to a great part of our lives: ' Ah! I have consumed my time in laboriously doing nothing!' "

How greatly does it exalt the mercy and goodness of the universal Parent of mankind, to perceive that his regard is equally towards his children and people, whatever may be their stations and conditions in the world! To the poor and illiterate, as well as to the rich and learned, the gospel is preached; and those of every class who become truly humble and poor in spirit, and those only, will cordially receive and rejoice in it. Learning and knowledge are, indeed, ornaments and improvements of our nature; and, as well as riches, rank, and influence enable us to enlarge the sphere of our utility and beneficence: but it is not hence to be inferred, either that these qualifications are not attended with peculiar dangers, temptations, and inquietudes, or, that the Father of spirits, who is just and equal in all his ways, regards their possessors with distinguished marks of his favor. The wisdom of Providence, to promote order and government in the earth, has, indeed, ordained a diversity of talents and conditions amongst men; but he has also graciously declared, that to the religious and faithful improvement, even of the fewest talents, shall be annexed the highest reward that can be conferred upon us; namely, that of " Well done, good and faithful servant; enter thou into the joy of thy Lord."

An humble and teachable disposition, a pious, upright, and benevolent temper of mind, are incomparably of greater worth, than all the accomplishments and possessions of the world; and they are the only attainments which. in all degrees of knowledge, and in every station and condition of life, will procure the Divine favor, and advance us to real honor and happiness.

SECTION IV.

MARGARET M. ALTHENS.

Margaret M. Althens, a person of great piety
and virtue, was born in the year 1752. It appears
that, from early life, she was favored with impressions of a religious nature; and that the awful
thoughts of heaven, hell, death, and eternity engrossed much of her attention. Her father died
when she was two and a half years old. Her mother being a German, she was educated in the language of that country, as well as in her native
tongue; and in the fifteenth year of her age, she
was confirmed in the German chapel by Dr. Wach-
sell. "I must acknowledge," says she, "that he
spared no pains to instruct me in the great principles of religion. But the endeavor of man cannot
reach the heart, unless influenced by the Spirit and
power of God. Though I was confirmed, and admitted a member of the congregation, I knew no
more what a change of heart meant, or an experimental knowledge of Jesus Christ, than one who
had never heard of him."

After this period she appears, by her Memoirs,
to have experienced great trials, temptations, and

mental distress. She became so deeply affected with the sense of her condition, that her heart was filled with despair. But it pleased the God of love and mercy to regard her with compassion, and to visit and strengthen her mind, by the gracious operations of his Holy Spirit. She was gradually enlightened, and enlarged in her religious views; and, at length, obtained an establishment in the paths of piety and virtue; and experienced a most consoling persuasion, that her heavenly Father would never forsake her.

The subject of this article, who possessed a cultivated mind, was brought up with pleasing expectations: but she participated in some of those vicissitudes which are so common in human life. For about seven years before her marriage, which took place in 1784, she lived in the capacity of a servant. This humble situation was, however, so sweetened and sanctified to her by the blessing of God, that, in several parts of her Diary, she expresses great thankfulness to him, for those dispensations of his providence, which, though painful at the time, were necessary to her spiritual improvement. She was thereby secluded from many temptations and snares, which she apprehended might otherwise have retarded her progress in the Christian life. Her state of dependence was, without doubt, less burdensome to her, because her trust was in the Lord whom she served.

The character of this excellent woman, who appears to have been happy in her marriage, is strongly portrayed in two letters which she wrote to her husband, and which appear to have been intended for his perusal, after her decease. We presume they will be acceptable to the reader. They contain great piety, great resignation, and a triumphant faith in the mercy and acceptance of her God and Redeemer. They exhibit a lively and animating example of true conjugal affection, and Christian desires for the best interests of a beloved partner, mingled with the joyful prospect of a blessed reunion of their spirits, in the mansions of eternal peace.

LETTER TO HER HUSBAND, NO. I.

My Most Dearly Beloved!

I frequently hear of the death of one and another in child-bed, which fills my mind with apprehensions; for what am I better than they, that I should expect more favor from the Lord?

The sun of prosperity has shone upon me for five years, and I have been blessed with one of the best of husbands; which makes the thought of the parting stroke most sensibly painful to me. If it were not for the great realities of religion, I could not give up the beloved of my heart. All the powers of my soul are at work, when I think what your feelings will be, in the trying hour of separation. But, my dearest, grieve not as without hope. When a few years more have finished their course, I trust, through the merits of the great Redeemer, that we shall have a happy meeting in our heavenly Father's house. Then, parting, sighs, and tears, shall be no more. Then, I humbly hope, we shall be for ever united, in singing the song of Moses and the Lamb.

The Almighty, who by a chain of providences brought us together, and only lent me to you for a short space, has an undoubted right to recall me when he pleases. Very pleasant hast thou been to me in life, and in death we shall not be divided. You will shed a tear to my memory, when you reflect on the many, yea, I may say, very many happy hours we have spent, and the endearing conversation we have had together. But the subject is too delicate; I must not dwell on it. Those seasons are now past. They are vanished, like the morning cloud, or early dew. Nothing now presents itself to me, but sorrow, anguish, weeping friends, the gloomy appendages of death, and an opening grave.

This is a dreary prospect; but, blessed be God, here it ends. Beyond the grave, the scenes are bright and happy. My reconciled God in Christ Jesus, will receive me, place a crown of glory upon my head, and fix my abode for ever among the sons of light. Angels wait their commission to conduct me to the New Jerusalem above; when, with a golden harp, and a palm of victory, I shall shine a monument of mercy.

There shall I wait the happy period of your arrival. Let this consideration restrain your tears: your sincerely affectionate wife is not dead, but sleepeth. You may commit my body to the ground, in sure and certain hope of a joyful resurrection. When you are performing the last kind offices of affection, I shall be rejoicing before the throne of God, drinking of the rivers of pleasure that are at his right hand.

If I should leave a helpless infant, you will take care of it, and let it be brought up with the rest, in the nurture and admonition of the Lord. I am not solicitous to have my children great; but it is my earnest wish and prayer, that they may be good. My beloved, press forward; a glorious prize awaits you. Be faithful unto death, and you shall obtain it. If you see me in my coffin, rejoice over me, and say: What was mortal, the worms shall destroy; but her soul, arrayed in the robe of the Redeemer's righteousness, lives, to die no more. Death is swallowed up in victory. We fall, we rise, we reign!

May the God of my youth, the protector of my advancing years, and the support of my now declining days, keep you under the shadow of his almighty wings! May he be your guard and guide through life, your comfort in the hour of dissolution, and your portion and happiness through the ages of eternity!

Your affectionate wife, in life and death,

M. M. A.

LETTER TO HER HUSBAND, NO. II.

MY MOST DEARLY BELOVED!

When you are reading these lines, there will be nothing left of me but a cold lump of clay. I bless God for having heard and answered my prayer, for, you know, I have often expressed a desire that my immortal spirit might take its flight before yours. Long may you live, for the sake of your dear family, to bring them up in the fear of the Lord! Let me entreat you not to sorrow as one without hope; for be assured that I am happy. I know that the enormous account of my sins is blotted out, by the precious blood of my crucified Redeemer; who came into the world to call, not the righteous, but such sinners as I am, to repentance: and he has declared, that where he is, his people shall also be. So that I am only transplanted from the church militant, into the church triumphant, to join with that general assembly, in praising the riches of redeeming grace and dying love.

I hope you have no doubt of the sincerity of my affection to you. Heaven is my witness, that your temporal and spiritual welfare has been the subject of my incessant prayers; and, I trust, they will be answered, when I am sleeping in the dust. If the disembodied spirits may be favored with the knowledge of things done below, and still interested in the concernments of their dear relatives, as I have some reason to think they will;—how gladly shall I accept the pleasing employ, of attending you as an invisible guardian angel, to warn you of dangers, and lend you aid in every season of distress! My first care should be, to wipe the tears from your beloved cheek; to soothe the wound my removal has made; and to help you to triumph over your loss, with the fortitude and resignation becoming you, as a child of God.

Time is short. In a few revolving years, at most, your silver cord of life will be loosed, and your golden bowl broken. Then, when every earthly comfort shall fade, you will know the worth of redemption, by the sufferings and death of the Son of God. O, that when flesh and heart shall fail, you may find him your strength and portion! If so, what a joyful meeting shall we have, to part no more; in his presence, where there is fulness of joy, and where all tears shall be wiped away!

I thank you for all the kindness you have shown to me, a most unworthy creature. You have indeed been a tender and affectionate husband to me. In you I have found a bosom friend; and my cares have been reposed in your beloved breast. My earthly happiness has been too great. I acquiesce. He who gave me life has a right to take it. I go to permanent happiness, without alloy, where sorrow can find no entrance.

And now, with all the solemn appendages of

death in my view; the gloomy grave, and an eter-
_nal world, into which I am about to enter; I lift
up my hands in supplication for you. May the
blessings of the eternal Jehovah rest upon you!
May his presence be your light and your strength,
to direct and support you, through all the changes
of this mortal life! And when you are bidding
adieu to all in this world, may his almighty arm be
your defence; and may his heavenly messengers
convey your departing spirit to the unsullied regions of eternal peace! Adieu! till we meet to
part no more. The Lord bless you!

Your affectionate wife,
M. M. A.

In the last illness of this truly religious person,
she was favored with an entire trust in God, and
with an earnest longing for that happy state, which
she believed was prepared for her. At one time
she says in her Diary: "I hope I can adopt the
language of Dr. Young :—

> "'Or life, or death, is equal; neither weighs.
> All weight in this—O! let me live to thee.'"

At another time she thus expresses herself: "I
am still under the care of a physician; but he gives
me no hope. Indeed it would be both cruel and
in vain to flatter me now; for my own weakness
informs me, that I am going apace. I bless my
God, I can now say, Thy will be done. I can give

up my dear husband and children, with every
earthly connection, into his hands. He will take
care of them. My husband's trial is great. I feel
more for him than for myself. But heaven will
make amends for all. O, how I pant and thirst for
the happy hour, when my Father will send his angels to convey my spirit to rest !"

She obtained her long desired release from sin
and sorrow, in the summer of the year 1789, and
at the age of thirty-seven years, within a few days.

SECTION V.

ZIMMERMAN.

THE following tribute to the memory of a beloved daughter, was written by Doctor Zimmerman; and marks the piety of his own mind, as well as the influence of religion on the amiable subject of his sorrow:

"May I be permitted here to give a short account of a young person, whose memory I am extremely anxious to preserve? The world was unacquainted with her excellence: she was known to those only whom she has left behind to bewail her loss. Her sole pleasures were those which a retired and virtuous life affords. She was active, invariably mild, and always compassionate to the miseries of others. Diffident of her own powers, she relied with perfect confidence on the goodness of God, and listened attentively to the precepts of a fond parent. Taught by my experience, submitting to my judgment, she entertained for me the most ardent affection; and convinced me, not by professions, but by actions, of her sincerity. Willingly would I have resigned my life to have saved hers; and I am satisfied that she would cheerfully have given up her own, to preserve mine. One of my greatest pleasures was, to please her; and my endeavors for that purpose were most gratefully returned. She gave many proofs of this kind and amiable temper: and I shall mention one, which, though small in itself, was peculiarly pleasing to me. She frequently presented me with a rose, which she knew was my favorite flower. I ever received it from her hand with delight, and preserved it as a rich treasure.

"From her earliest infancy, she had been the submissive victim of ill health. But though of a weak frame of body, and very deeply afflicted, she bore her sufferings with steady fortitude, and pious resignation to the dispensation of Heaven. Her appetite was almost gone when we left Switzerland; a residence which, though peculiarly endeared to her, she quitted with her usual sweetness of temper, and without discovering the smallest regret.

"Soon after our arrival at Hanover, she fell into a deep decline, which at length terminated in a hemorrhage of the lungs, of a very uncommon nature, that soon deprived me of the comfort of this beloved child. From the knowledge I had of her constitution, I apprehended that the disorder would prove mortal. How frequently, during that fatal day, did my wounded, bleeding heart, bend me on my knees before God, to supplicate for her recovery! But I concealed my feelings from her observation.

"Although sensible of her danger, she never discovered the least apprehension. Smiles played around her pallid cheeks, whenever I entered or quitted the room. Though worn down by the fatal distemper, a prey to the most corroding sorrows, the sharpest and most afflicting pains, she made no complaint. She mildly answered all my questions, by some short sentence, without entering into any details. Her decay and impending dissolution became obvious to the eye; but to the last moment of her life, her countenance preserved a serenity correspondent to the purity of her mind, and the tender emotions of her heart. Thus I beheld my dear, my only daughter, at the age of five-and-twenty, after a tedious suffering of nine long months, expire in my arms.

"During the short time we passed at Hanover, where she was much respected and beloved, she amused herself by composing several religious pieces, which were afterwards found among her papers; and in which she implores death to afford her a speedy relief from her pains. About the same period, she wrote also many letters, which were always affecting, and frequently sublime. They were filled with expressions of the same desire, speedily to unite her soul with the Author of her being. The last words that my dear, my excellent child uttered, amidst the most painful agonies, were these: 'To-day I shall taste the joys of heaven!'"

SECTION VI.

JAMES HAY BEATTIE.

James Hay Beattie, son of Dr. James Beattie, professor of moral philosophy and logic in the university of Aberdeen, was born in the year 1768. He died early in life at the age of twenty-two; but wisdom, not years, is the grey hair to man, and unspotted life is old age.

This young man possessed a fine genius, great vigor of understanding, and a very uncommon portion of learning and knowledge: but the rectitude of heart, and genuine piety, by which he was so eminently distinguished, are the qualities which render him a proper subject for these memoirs.

We shall select a few traits of the life and character of this excellent youth, as proofs of his uncommon merit, and of the power of religion on his mind.

His father never had occasion to reprove him above three or four times, during the whole of his life: bodily chastisement he never experienced at all. It would indeed have been most unreasonable to apply this mode of discipline to one whose supreme concern it ever was to know his duty, and

to do it. The first rules of morality which his father taught him, were, to speak truth, and keep a
secret; and it never appeared that in a single instance, he transgressed either. His whole behavior, at school and college, was not only irreproachable, but exemplary.

In the year 1787, the king, upon the recommendation of the university of Marischal college,
was pleased to appoint him assistant professor of
moral philosophy and logic. His age was then not
quite nineteen; but to the gentlemen of the university his character was so well known, that they
most readily, as well as unanimously, concurred in
the recommendation. His steadiness, good-nature,
and self-command, secured his authority as a
teacher: and by his presence of mind, and ready
recollection, he satisfied his audience that, though
young, he was abundantly qualified to instruct
them.

Piety and meekness were striking features in his
character, habitual to him in infancy, and through
life. The Christian religion and its evidences he
had studied with indefatigable application; and
the consequence was such as may always be expected in like cases, where the inquirer has candor
and sense: no person could love his religion more
than he did, or believe in it with fuller assurance
of faith. But in his behaviour there was no aus-
terity or singularity. The effect of religion upon
his mind was, to make him cheerful, considerate,

benevolent, intrepid, humble, and happy. He loved the whole human race ; he bore a particular love to Christians ; and he wished all parties to exercise Christian charity towards each other. He wished to be, and to be considered, a Christian ; a title which he thought infinitely more honorable than any other.

The purity and the delicacy of his mind were great ; and in one so young, were truly admirable, and worthy of imitation. He was aware of the danger of admitting indelicate or improper thoughts into his mind ; for he knew that associations of ideas, disapproved both by reason as incongruous, and by conscience as immoral, might in a moment be formed, in consequence of inadvertence, even when there was no settled propensity to evil. His attention was continually awake to learn, although from the slightest hint, or most trivial circumstance, what might be useful in purifying his mind, regulating his conduct, or improving his understanding.

He was almost constantly occupied in discharging the duties of his office, in performing acts of kindness, or in planning works of literature for the benefit of mankind ; and there is every reason to believe, that if his life had been lengthened, he would have been eminently useful in the world. But it pleased Divine Providence to permit this promising youth to be cut down by disease, in the morning of life. When his disorder had made

great progress, and he saw death approaching, he
met it with his usual calmness and resignation.
One evening, while he was expecting the physician,
who had been sent for in the belief that he was
just going to expire, he sweetly said: "How pleasant a medicine is Christianity!"

He sometimes endeavored to reconcile his father's mind to the thought of parting with him;
but, for fear of giving him pain, spoke seldom and
sparingly on that subject. "One day," says his
father, "when I was sitting by him, he began to
speak in very affectionate terms, as he often had
done, of what he called my goodness to him. I
begged him to drop that subject; and was pro-
ceeding to tell him, that I had never done anything for him but what my duty required, and inclination prompted; and that, for the little I had
done, his filial piety and other virtues were to me
more than a sufficient recompense,—when he interrupted me, (which he was not apt to do,) and,
starting up, with inexpressible fervor and solemnity, implored the blessing of God upon me. His
look at that moment, though I shall never forget
it, I can describe in no other way than by saying,
that it seemed to have in it something more than
human, and what I may not very improperly, perhaps, call angelic. Seeing me agitated, he expressed concern for what he had done—and said
that whatever might be in his mind, he would not
any more put my feelings to so severe a trial

Sometimes, however, warm sentiments of gratitude would break from him: and those were the only occasions on which, during the whole course of his illness, he was observed to shed tears, till the day before his death; when he desired to see his brother, gave him his blessing, wept over him, and bid him farewell."

The preceding traits of the life and virtues of this amiable and accomplished youth, are taken from an account of his life and character, written and published by his very worthy father, Dr. James Beattie; to which publication the compiler refers the reader for further particulars. He will find it a well-written, instructive, and most interesting detail of the sentiments and conduct of this excellent young man.

We cannot better close this memoir, than by transcribing the pious and pathetic lines of his father, at the conclusion of that work: "I have lost the pleasantest, and, for the last four or five years of his short life, one of the most instructive companions, that ever man was delighted with. But, ' the Lord gave; the Lord hath taken away: blessed be the name of the Lord.'—I adore the Author of all Good, who gave him grace to lead such a life, and die such a death, as makes it impossible for a Christian to doubt of his having entered upon the inheritance of a happy immortality."

SECTION VII.

ELIZABETH SMITH.

THIS amiable and excellent person was born at Burnhall in the county of Durham, in the year 1776, at which place her parents then resided, in affluent circumstances, though afterwards they experienced a reverse of fortune. At a very early age, she discovered that love of reading, and that close application to whatever she engaged in, which marked her character through life. She was accustomed, when only three years old, to leave an elder brother and younger sister to play and amuse themselves, whilst she eagerly seized on such books as a nursery library commonly affords, and made herself mistress of their contents. At four years of age, she read extremely well; and, from the judicious account which her mother gives of her, it appears, that whatever she did was *well done*, and with an apparent consideration far beyond her years.

As she grew up, she was remarkable for a thirst of knowledge, for regularity, and observation. Her person and manners were highly pleasing, and her disposition was mild and benevolent. She had a pensive softness of countenance, that indicated deep reflection ; but her extreme timidity concealed, for a time, the very extraordinary talents which she possessed. She was instructed, and made great progress in the accomplishments which are usually taught to females in the polished circles of life. But she was eminently distinguished for a love of learning, a facility in acquiring languages, and a desire to improve her mind. With scarcely any assistance, she taught herself the French, Italian, Spanish, German, Latin, Greek, and Hebrew languages: and she had no inconsiderable knowledge of Arabic and Persic. She was well acquainted with geometry, algebra, and other branches of the mathematics.

" With all these acquirements," says her excellent biographer, " she was perfectly feminine in her disposition ; elegant, modest, gentle, and affectionate : nothing was neglected which a woman ought to know ; no duty was omitted, which her situation in life required her to perform. But the part of her character on which," continues her biographer, " I dwell with the greatest satisfaction, is that exalted piety, which seemed always to raise her above this world ; and taught her, at sixteen years of age, to resign its riches and its pleasures, almost without regret, and to support with dignity a very unexpected change of situation.

" For some years before her death, the Holy Scripture was her principal study ; and she translated from the Hebrew the whole book of Job, &c., &c. The benefit which she herself derived from these studies, must be evident to those who witnessed the patience and resignation with which she supported a long and painful illness, the sweet attention which she always showed to the feelings of her parents and friends, and the heavenly composure with which she looked forward to the awful change, which has now removed her to a world ' where,' as one of her friends observes, ' her gentle, pure, and enlightened spirit will find itself more at home, than in this land of shadows.' "

This pious and admirable young person, was not destined by Divine Providence to continue long on this stage of probation and conflict. In the summer of 1805, she caught a cold, which, though at first it seemed not to be of much consequence, gradually impaired her constitution ; so that, in little more than a year from the commencement of the disorder, her valuable life was terminated. She finished her course in the thirtieth year of her age.

After her death, there was found amongst her manuscripts, a number of reflections on a variety of important subjects, moral and religious. We shall select a few of these, and present them to the reader, as interesting specimens of the goodness both of her head and her heart :

"Pleasure is a rose near which there ever grows the thorn of evil. It is wisdom's work so carefully to cull the rose, as to avoid the thorn, and let its rich perfume exhale to heaven in grateful adoration of Him who gave the rose to blow.

"The Christian life may be compared to a magnificent column, whose summit always points to heaven. The innocent and therefore real pleasures of this world are the ornaments on the pedestal; very beautiful and highly to be enjoyed, when the eye is near; but which should not too long, or too frequently detain us from that just distance, where we can contemplate the whole column, and where the ornaments on its base disappear.

"How light are all the troubles of this world, to those who value everything it contains, according to its real worth! They may appear insensible, to those who reckon by a different standard; but they can bear even this imputation, for they know the value of human applause. How happy should we be, if we could always *feel*, as we *sometimes think!*

"No event which I thought unfortunate has ever happened to me, but I have been convinced, at some time or other, that it was not a misfortune, but a blessing. I can never then in reason complain of anything that happens, because I am persuaded it is permitted for some good purpose.

"An hour well spent condemns a life. When we reflect on the sum of improvement and delight gained in that single hour, how do the multitude of hours already past, rise up and say, what good has marked us? Wouldst thou know the true worth of time, *employ one hour.*"

The following lines, contained in a little pocket-book, and written by her in the year 1798, when she had attained the age of twenty-one years, are peculiarly interesting. They indicate the deep sense which she had of the value and importance of religion:

"Being now arrived at what is called years of discretion, and looking back on my past life with shame and confusion, when I recollect the many advantages I have had, and the bad use I have made of them, the hours I have squandered, and the opportunities of improvement I have neglected; when I imagine what, with those advantages, I ought to be, and find myself what I am:—I am resolved to endeavor to be more careful, for the future, if the future be granted me; to try to make amends for past negligence, by employing every moment I can command, to some good purpose; to endeavor to acquire all the little knowledge that human nature is capable of on earth; but to let the word of God be my chief study, and all others subservient to it; to model myself as far as I am able, according to the Gospel of Christ; to be content while my trial lasts, and when it is finished, to rejoice, trusting in the merits of my Redeemer. I have written these resolutions, to stand as a witness against me, in case I should be inclined to forget them, and to return to my former insolence and thoughtlessness, because I have found the inutility of mental determinations. May God grant me strength to keep them!"

These pious and holy resolutions, were, we presume, succeeded by great watchfulness against temptations, and by devout and earnest endeavors to secure the momentous and happy objects which she had in view. Her trials and conflicts are all over; and she is gone to receive, through Divine grace, the reward of her virtues. But her example still remains; and to those by whom it is duly contemplated, it may prove a powerful incentive, to imitate her goodness, and to aspire after that future blessedness, which animated her hopes and exertions.

SECTION VIII.

ELIZABETH CARTER.

ELIZABETH CARTER, a person highly estimable for her learning, talents, and virtues, was born at Deal, in the year 1717. Her father, Dr. Nicholas Carter, a clergyman in Kent, was a man of great learning, and of exemplary character. He gave all his children, daughters as well as sons, a learned education. But the infancy and early youth of Elizabeth afforded no promise of the attainments which she afterwards acquired. Yet even then, it was her most eager desire to be a scholar, though nature seemed to forbid it.

She gained the rudiments of knowledge with great labor and difficulty; and her perseverance was put to a most severe trial. This ardent thirst after knowledge, was, however, at length crowned with complete success; and her acquirements became, even very early in life, such as are rarely met with. Her proficiency in languages was very extraordinary, for her age and sex. Besides Latin, Greek, and Hebrew, she became possessed of the French, Italian, Spanish, and German tongues; the last three of which she attained without a master.

Poetry was one of her early tastes; and in 1738 she published a small collection of Poems, written before she was twenty years of age. The sciences were not neglected by her. She paid great attention to Astronomy; which she thought a noble study, and in which she made a very considerable progress. She gained such a knowledge of history, both ancient and modern, as is rarely acquired; and her taste for that engaging, as well as useful branch of science, she never lost. Yet, amidst her various applications and employments, she found time to work a great deal with her needle, not only for herself, but also for the family. She was not inattentive to domestic economy, and the occupations that belong to the female character.

"But among her studies, there was one which she never neglected; one which was always dear to her, from her earliest infancy to the latest period of her life, and in which she made a continual improvement. This was that of Religion, which was her constant care, and greatest delight. Her acquaintance with the Bible, some part of which she never failed to read every day, was as complete, as her belief in it was sincere. And no person ever endeavored more, and few with greater success, to regulate the whole of their conduct by that unerring guide. Her piety was indeed the very piety of the Gospel, shown not by enthusiasm, or depreciating that of others; but by a calm, rational, and constant devotion, and the most unwearied attention to acquire the temper, and practise the duties of a Christian life. She never thanked God, like the proud Pharisee, that she was not like others; but rather, like the Publican, besought him to be merciful to her, a sinner.

"She admired, and warmly felt, the beauties of works of genius and fancy; but in her estimation, *the one thing needful*, duty to God and man, in its highest sense, superseded all the rest. Hence the works of art, and the beauties of nature, equally turned her thoughts in gratitude to Him, who has granted us faculties and senses capable of giving and receiving so much innocent pleasure."

This excellent woman had a heart finely adapted to friendship; and she possessed many friends of distinguished character, who proved the instruments of much enjoyment to her. In particular, she formed an intimate connection with the accomplished Catherine Talbot, who was niece to the lord chancellor Talbot, and who possessed considerable genius, and a most amiable disposition. This was an important event in the life of Elizabeth Carter. The intimacy of their friendship, the interesting nature of their correspondence, and the exalted piety of both, rendered this connection the principal ingredient of their mutual happiness. It procured also the friendship of Dr. Secker, archbishop of Canterbury, with whom her beloved Catherine resided.

Under these favorable circumstances, she extended her knowledge of the world, cherished her profound learning, and exercised her pious views and sentiments. It was by the desire of this valued female friend, enforced by the bishop of Oxford, that she undertook the work, by which her literary reputation has been most known abroad, and will be long remembered by scholars at home, her translation of Epictetus.

She was, for many years, happy in her union and intercourse with a woman so very dear to her: and when the time of their separation came, it was, as may be supposed, an event deeply affecting to her susceptible mind. From a letter which she wrote, on this melancholy occasion, we extract the following passages: "Never surely was there a more perfect pattern of evangelical goodness, decorated by all the ornaments of a highly improved understanding; and recommended by a sweetness of temper, and an elegance and politeness of manners of a peculiar and more engaging kind, in any other character I ever knew. Little, alas! infinitely too little have I yet profited by the blessing of such an example. God grant that her memory, which I hope will ever survive in my heart, may produce a happier effect. Adieu, my dear friend. God bless you; and conduct us both to that happy assembly, where the spirits of the just shall dread no future separation! And may we both remember that awful truth, that we can hope to die the death of the righteous only by resembling their lives."

The subject of this memoir survived her lamented friend many years: and it appears that her lamp continued to burn brightly, till there was no fuel left to supply it.

" About nine years before her death, she returned from London at her usual time, much disordered by a complaint which was supposed to be the Saint Anthony's Fire. In the course of the summer she was reduced by it to the lowest extremity; and was given over by her medical attendants, and by all her friends. She thought herself going, and was prepared for the important change. Though her strength failed, her spirits never flagged, and she spoke of her approaching departure, with the most pious hope and resignation, and even with cheerfulness. Her life, she said, had been a prosperous and happy one, and if it seemed fit to God she would be glad to live longer: if it was his pleasure to take her, she was ready and willing to depart; and trusted to his mercies, through Christ, for the forgiveness of her sins. It pleased God, however, that she should return from the very verge of the grave; but her recovery was slow, and incomplete at best; and she never recovered her former strength."

At length, the period approached, when this distinguished person was to take her final leave of all transitory objects. Her strength gradually wasted; and to most of her friends it was evident, that she was journeying slowly, but surely, towards *the house appointed for all living.* Yet " her piety

was as fervent, her temper as mild, and her wishes
for those she loved as warm, as in the time of her
strong health." She retained her senses till within
a few hours of her decease: which took place in
the winter of the year 1806, and in the eighty-ninth
year of her age.

A few extracts from the writings of this truly
valuable woman, will further evince the excellence
of her religious principles; the piety and devotion
of her mind; and her entire resignation to the will
of her heavenly Father.

THOUGHTS ON THE PRESENT STATE OF AFFAIRS, 1752.

The last winter has been a calamitous one to several nations, and alarming to our own; and the
summer prospect is clouded with impending dangers. What method can I take to avoid the
threatened evil, or to quiet my fears? Can I fly
into some distant country, and endeavor to secure
myself there? My connections and attachments
render this an impracticable scheme. Shall I depend for protection on the assistance of my friends?
They are helpless and defenceless as myself. Is
there then no refuge left? Yes; a reliance on
Him, in whose hand are the *issues of life and death*,
and the disposal of all events.

And have I then been careful to secure an interest in this Almighty Protector, this unfailing

friend? Dare I, with humble hope and confidence, look up for aid and support to that God, who *is of purer eyes than to behold iniquity?* This is an awful and important inquiry, and merits my most serious attention. Let me examine my own heart. Of atrocious crimes perhaps it fully acquits me: but to these have I any temptation? In avoiding them, how little have I to boast! But are there not faults of a less observable nature, and often much too slightly overlooked, for which, in my situation, I am strictly accountable? By the gracious dispensation of Providence, I am a Christian; have I duly considered what this sacred character imports? what a strictness of behavior my profession requires? Is religion, and a perpetual view to the solemn account which I must one day render, the governing principle of my life? Does it, as far as mortal frailty will permit, influence my whole conduct, my actions, my discourses, and accompany me even in my diversions and amusements?

In this season of public danger, let me consider in what particulars I am faulty; and sincerely endeavor, by the Divine assistance, to correct what I discover to be wrong.

Fear, when it terminates in itself, is a painful and contemptible passion; but, properly applied, may be sanctified to a noble use. That use, our blessed Saviour has pointed out to me. If the fear of God influences me to correct whatever would tend to deprive me of his favor and protection, what else shall I have to fear? Whatever be the event of the present alarming dangers to me, if I do not forfeit my hope in the Divine Goodness, it will certainly be happy. Though the earth trembles beneath my feet, my soul will be immoveably fixed on *the Rock of Ages;* and when the sword hangs over my head, I shall *acquaint myself with God, and be at peace.*

EXTRACT FROM A LETTER TO ———.

To consider the Gospel merely as a subject of speculation, which we are at liberty to examine, or let alone, just as our other avocations will allow, is not having such a sense of its awful importance, as gives room to expect any satisfaction from the inquiry. To examine it more diligently, and more in earnest, yet entirely with a confidence in our own understanding, is not having a proper sense of human weakness. Religion is a most solemn transaction between God and the soul, founded on every relation in which we stand to him; and it is only by keeping up a perpetual intercourse with him, and by an endeavor to form not only our outward behavior, but the whole internal frame of our mind, with a reference to his approbation, that we can become sufficiently divested of all wrong tendencies, to be duly qualified to judge of the truth of any revelation proposed in his name.

Those who sincerely wish to make his will the

first object of their choice, who submit their understanding to his direction, and implore and depend on his assistance to guard them from error, his goodness will never suffer to be fatally misled : and they will enter on their inquiry with a full security of obtaining every degree of conviction which is necessary to their virtue and their peace. So true, I believe, is the position that conviction depends on the heart, that I think you will not, in the whole circle of your observation, find a single instance of a person whose heart was disposed in the manner which I have described, who ever continued an unbeliever.

ON THE OCCASION OF MAKING HER WILL.

In the solemn act of making one's last will, something surely ought to be added to the mere forms of law. Upon this occasion, which is a kind of taking leave of the world, I acknowledge with gratitude and thanksgiving, how much I owe to the Divine Goodness, for a life distinguished by innumerable and unmerited blessings.

Next to God, the supreme and original author of all happiness, I desire to express my thankfulness to those whom he has made the instruments of conveying his benefits to me. Most particularly I am indebted to my father, for his kindness and indulgence to me, in every instance, and especially in the uncommon care and pains he has taken in

my education; which has been the source of such
a variety of reasonable pleasures, as well as of very
great advantages in my conversation with the
world.

I likewise very heartily thank my mother,* my
brothers and sisters, for all the instances of kindness and affection, by which they have contributed
to the comfort of my life. If, in this disposition of
my affairs, I appear to have made any distinction,
I entreat them to believe, that not any difference
in my own good-will to them, but a regard to their
different circumstances, has been the real motive
of it.

Besides my own family, there are very many
others, to whom I have been obliged, for very considerable advantages, in the assistance and pleasures of friendship. Of these I retain a most affectionate and grateful memory; and desire all my
intimate friends to consider themselves as included
in my sincere acknowledgments.

And now, O gracious God, whether it be thy
will to remove me speedily from the world, or to
allot me a longer time in it, on Thee alone I depend for happiness both here and hereafter. I acknowledge my own unworthiness, and that all my
claim to thy favor is founded on thy infinite goodness in the merciful dispensation of the Gospel. I
implore the pardon of all my sins, and humbly
hope for those pleasures which are at thy right

* Her mother-in-law, who was then living.

hand for evermore, in and through Him by whom all thy blessings are conveyed, my blessed Lord, Redeemer, and only Saviour, Jesus Christ.

ELIZABETH CARTER.

February 9, 1759.

A MORNING PRAYER.

O God, my merciful Father, I humbly thank Thee for preserving me in safety the past night, for refreshing me with quiet sleep, and raising me in health and peace, to the enjoyment of a world which Thou hast made so beautiful, and in which Thou hast allotted me such innumerable mercies. I bless thee for all the comforts of my life; for health and plenty, good parents, kind relations, and kind friends; I beg of Thee to bless and reward them, and to make me dutiful and grateful to them.

Under a sense of my own weakness, I beg the assistance of thy Holy Spirit, to enable me to resist the dangerous temptations and bad examples of the world, the wrong dispositions of my own heart and temper, and the snares of Satan. I humbly beseech Thee to take my inexperienced youth under thy protection. Keep me, O Lord, from presumption and vanity; from idle dissipation, and extravagant expenses. Impress on my soul a constant regard to that awful account of all my thoughts, words, and actions, which I must give to

Thee, at the dreadful day of judgment. Grant me
a firm persuasion, that all my peace of mind here,
and my happiness hereafter, must depend on my
improvement in piety and in the duties of a Christian life. Teach me to rely with perfect dependence upon Thee, who alone knowest what is truly
good for me, and dispose me to cheerful contentment, in whatever condition Thou seest fit to
place me.

I beseech Thee to guard me this day from all
danger, particularly from the greatest of all evils,
the doing any thing displeasing to Thee. I humbly offer up all my petitions in the name, and
through the intercession, of my blessed Saviour,
who has taught me, when I pray, to say, Our
Father, &c.

We shall close the memoir of this pious and
distinguished female with an honorable testimony
to her talents and character, as well as to those of
Elizabeth Smith, selected from one of the publications of the celebrated Hannah More:

" Against learning, against talents of any kind,
othing can steady the head, unless you fortify the
.eart with real Christianity. In raising the moral
edifice we must sink deep in proportion as we
build high. We must widen the foundation, if we
xtend the superstructure. Religion alone can
ounteract the aspirings of genius, can regulate the

pride of talents. And yet such women as are disposed to be vain of their comparatively petty attainments, look up with admiration to those contemporary shining examples, the venerable Elizabeth Carter, and the blooming Elizabeth Smith.' I knew them both; and to know, was to revere them. In them let our young ladies contemplate profound and various learning, chastised by true Christian humility. In them, let them venerate acquirements, which would have been distinguished in a university, meekly softened, and beautifully shaded, by the gentle exertion of every domestic virtue; the unaffected exercise of every feminine employment."

SECTION IX.

SIR WILLIAM JONES.

Sir William Jones, an eminent lawyer, and most accomplished scholar, was born in London, in the year 1746. He lost his father when he was only three years of age; and the care of his education devolved on his mother, a woman of uncommon mental endowments. She was very solicitous to kindle in his young mind a love for reading; which she effected, by constantly replying to those questions that a native ardor for instruction incessantly prompted, "Read, and you will know." This he did to a great extent, at a very early period.

He was not one of those happy geniuses, (if such there are,) who can make brilliant acquisitions without pains. It was, on the contrary, by the most sedulous industry, and the renunciation of the usual diversions of a school-boy, joined with the natural gift of a very retentive memory, that he was enabled to lay in those ample stores of knowledge, by which he became so highly distinguished.

In 1764, he was entered of University college, Oxford; and his excellent mother, who devoted her time almost entirely to him, fixed her residence in the same city. This affectionate and judicious attention must have preserved him from many dangers, and was doubtless productive of great comfort and advantage to him. He ever regarded her with true filial affection and gratitude; and the desire of relieving her from the burden of his education, rendered a fellowship in the college the great object of his wishes. This soon fell into his possession, and placed him, according to his own idea, in a state of independence. He had the private tuition of young Lord Althorpe, now Earl Spencer; with whom he made a tour to the continent, by which he was introduced into the most respectable company, and derived not only amusement, but much instruction.

As he was desirous of obtaining a station in society adequate to his endowments, and by which he might be, in no ordinary degree, useful to his fellow-creatures, he chose the profession of law, for the study of which he had acquired a particular predilection. He entered at the Temple in the year 1770; and four years afterwards he was called to the Bar. He did not, however, sacrifice to professional studies all those literary pursuits which had so delightfully occupied him. He published several volumes of poems, partly translations from the poets of Asia, and a number of critical dissertations, which attracted the notice and admiration of persons, both at home and abroad, who were competent judges of the subjects.

The post of one of the judges in the English territories of India, had long been a particular object of his wishes, principally on account of the opportunity it would afford him of gratifying his ardent desire of oriental researches. And in 1783, he received the appointment of a judge of the supreme court of judicature at Fort William, in Bengal; and at the same time the honor of knighthood was conferred upon him. About this period, he married a most amiable woman, whose cultivated mind and excellent heart, were finely adapted to his views and happiness.

The field of action and enquiry which opened to him in India, was immense. He planned the institution of a society in Calcutta, similar to the Royal Society of London; and the labors and discoveries of this institution have been very interesting and eminently useful. For his extensive researches into the history, laws, literature, and religion of India, the world is greatly indebted to him; and from them the cause of Christianity has derived no inconsiderable aid.

This learned and excellent man was, in the prime of his days, and when apparently in good health, seized with a disorder which, in about a week, put a period to his valuable life. His biographer, Lord Teignmouth, observes, that "the progress of the complaint was uncommonly rapid, and terminated fatally on the 27th of April, 1794. On the morning of that day, his attendants, alarmed at the evident symptoms of approaching dissolution, came precipitately to call the friend who has now the melancholy task of recording the mournful event: not a moment was lost in repairing to his house. He was lying on his bed in a posture of meditation; and the only symptom of remaining life, was a small degree of motion in the heart, which after a few seconds ceased, and he expired without a pang or groan. His bodily suffering, from the complacence of his features and the ease of his attitude, could not have been severe; and his mind must have derived consolation from those sources, where he had been in the habit of seeking it, and where alone, in our last moments, it can ever be found."

When Sir William Jones was visited with his last illness, he was in the forty-eighth year of his age, possessing the full vigor of his mental powers, and occupied with vast projects of literature, which might have employed an active life protracted to the utmost limits allotted to the human race. Few men have died more respected, or more regretted, and few have passed a more useful and irreproachable life.

The vast extent of his erudition has been displayed in his literary labors; to which it may be added, that scarcely any subject of human research escaped his notice. As a linguist, he has rarely, if ever, been equalled; for his list of languages comprehends, " eight studied critically; eight studied less perfectly, but all intelligible with a dictionary; and twelve studied least perfectly, but all attainable." His industry in acquiring elementary knowledge was not, however, productive of dryness: taste and elegance marked all his exertions. As a poet, he would probably have risen to the first class, had his ardor for transplanting foreign beauties allowed him leisure for the exercise of his own invention.

His private virtues were not inferior to his intellectual endowments. As a son, a husband, a friend, and a citizen, he fulfilled every duty in an exemplary manner. His integrity in the exercises of his judicial office was above all suspicion. He was totally free from pedantry, as well as from that arrogance and self-sufficiency which sometimes accompany and disgrace the greatest abilities. His presence was the delight of every society which his conversation exhilarated and improved; and his whole conduct bespoke a manly and independent spirit. A rational and exalted piety crowned the whole of his great attainments, and excellent qualities.

"The mind of Sir William Jones," says his pious and elegant biographer, "was never tainted with infidelity. But there was a period, before his judgment was matured, and before he had studied the Scriptures with close attention, when his belief in the truth of Revelation was tinged with doubts. But these were the transient clouds, which, for a while, obscure the dawn, and disperse with the rising sun. His heart and his judgment told him, that religion is a subject of supreme importance, and the evidence of its truth worthy of his most serious investigation. He sat down to the enquiry without prejudice, and rose from it with a conviction which the studies of his future life invigorated and confirmed. The completion of the prophecies relating to our Saviour, had impressed upon his youthful mind, this invaluable truth, that the language of Isaiah, and other prophets, was inspired; and in this belief, to which fresh proofs were progressively added, he closed his life. He has, I trust, received, through the merits of his Redeemer, the reward of his faith.

"In matters of eternal concern, the authority of the highest human opinions has no claim to be admitted, as a ground of belief; but it may, with the strictest propriety, be opposed to that of men of inferior learning and penetration; and whilst the pious derive satisfaction from the perusal of sentiments according with their own, those who doubt or disbelieve, should be induced to weigh, with candor and impartiality, arguments which have produced conviction in the minds of the best, the wisest, and the most learned of mankind.

"Among such as have professed a steady belief in the doctrine of Christianity, where shall greater names be found than those of Bacon and Newton? Of the former, and of Locke, it may be observed, that they were both innovators in science: disdaining to follow the sages of antiquity through the beaten paths of error, they broke through prejudices which had long obstructed the progress of sound knowledge, and they laid the foundation of science on solid ground; whilst the genius of Newton led him to discoveries of an amazing extent.

"These men, to their great praise, and we may hope to their eternal happiness, devoted much of their time to the study of the Scriptures. If the evidence of Revelation had been weak, who were better qualified to expose its unsoundness? Why were minds which boldly destroyed the prejudices in science, blind to those in religion? They read, examined, weighed, and believed; and the same vigorous intellect, that dispersed the mists which concealed the temple of human knowledge, was itself illuminated with the radiant truths of Divine Revelation. Such authorities, and let me now subjoin to them the name of Sir William Jones, are deservedly entitled to great estimation.

"In some of his papers, containing a delineation of his *daily* occupations, I find a portion of his time allotted to the perusal of the Scriptures. And I am authorized to add, not only from what appears in his printed works and private memoranda, but from particular and satisfactory testimony, that the writings of our best divines engaged a large share of his attention; and that

private devotion was not neglected by him. The
following lines, which afford a proof both of his
taste and piety, were written by him in the year
1786, after a perusal of the eighth sermon of
Barrow :

"' As meadows parch'd, brown groves, and withering flow'rs,
  Imbibe the sparkling dew and genial show'rs ;
  As chill dark air inhales the morning beam ;
  As thirsty hearts enjoy the gelid stream ;
  Thus to man's grateful soul, from heaven, descend
  The mercies of his Father, Lord, and Friend.'"

Sir William Jones, in his Bible, wrote the following note; which, coming from a man of his
profound erudition, and perfect knowledge of the
oriental languages, customs, and manners, must
be considered as a powerful testimony, not only to
the sublimity, but to the Divine inspiration, of the
sacred Scriptures :

"I have," says he, "carefully and regularly
perused these holy Scriptures; and am of opinion
that the volume, independently of its Divine ori-
gin, contains more sublimity, purer morality, more
important history, and finer strains of eloquence,
than can be collected from all other books, in whatever language they may have been written."

As religion was the subject of his meditations
in health, it was more forcibly impressed upon his
mind during illness. He knew the duty of resignation to the will of his Maker, and of dependence
on the merits of a Redeemer. These sentiments

are expressed in a short prayer, which he composed during his indisposition in 1784; and which is in the following words:

"O thou Bestower of all good! if it please thee to continue my easy tasks in this life, grant me strength to perform them as a faithful servant: but if thy wisdom hath willed to end them by this thy visitation, admit me, not weighing my unworthiness, but through thy mercy declared in Christ, into thy heavenly mansions, that I may continually advance in happiness, by advancing in true knowledge and awful love of thee. Thy will be done!"

Another short prayer, composed by him, on waking one morning at sea during the voyage to India, is worthy of insertion:

"Graciously accept our thanks, thou Giver of all good, for having preserved us another night, and bestowed on us another day. O, grant that on this day we may meditate on thy law with joyful veneration; and keep it in all our actions, with firm obedience."

Amongst the papers written by this truly excellent man, was a prayer, composed by him on the first day of the year 1782, about twelve years before his death. It is evidently the effusion of a pious mind, deeply impressed with an awful sense of the infinite wisdom, power, and benevolence of his Creator; and of the ignorance, weakness, and depravity of human nature. It contains sublime views of the Divine attributes; and the most humble dependence on God, for light and ability to serve him acceptably. The following passages are selected from this solemn and devout composition:

"Eternal and Incomprehensible Mind, who, by thy boundless power, before time began, createdst innumerable worlds for thy glory, and innumerable orders of beings for their happiness, which thy infinite goodness prompted Thee to desire, and thy infinite wisdom enabled Thee to know! we, thy creatures, vanish into nothing before thy supreme Majesty. To thy power we humbly submit; of thy goodness we devoutly implore protection; on thy wisdom we firmly and cheerfully rely. Irradiate our minds with all useful truth; instil into our hearts a spirit of general benevolence; give understanding to the foolish; meekness to the proud; temperance to the dissolute; fortitude to the feeble-hearted; hope to the desponding; faith to the unbelieving; diligence to the slothful; patience to those who are in pain; and thy celestial aid to those who are in danger: comfort the afflicted; relieve the distressed; supply the hungry with salutary food, and the thirsty with a plentiful stream. Impute not our doubts to indifference, nor our slowness of belief to hardness of heart; but be indulgent to our imperfect nature, and supply our imperfections by thy heavenly favor.

"Whenever we address thee in our retirement from the vanities of the world, if our prayers are foolish, pity us; if presumptuous, pardon us; if acceptable to thee, grant them, all-powerful God, grant them! And as, with our living voice, and with our dying lips, we will express our submission to thy decrees, adore thy providence, and bless thy dispensations; so, in all future states, to which we reverently hope thy goodness will raise us, grant that we may continue praising, admiring, venerating, worshipping thee more and more, through worlds without number, and ages without end."

CONCLUSION.

The Reader, before he closes this volume, will naturally pause, and encourage reflections adapted to the subject. He has been presented with the testimonies and experience of a number of his fellow-creatures, of different periods, countries, professions, and situations in life. He has found them all uniting in their attestation to the power and excellence of true religion, as our surest guide and consolation through time, and the only means of securing eternal happiness.

This solemn and concurrent testimony is of great importance. Much of it proceeds from some of the most eminent persons that have ever appeared in the world, whether we consider their station, their abilities, or their virtue. It is on a subject of the most interesting nature: and claims our serious and reverent attention, as the sentiments of men, who were too much enlightened to be deceived themselves, and too deeply affected, as well as too virtuous, to deceive others. They expressed their genuine feelings, and their unbiassed views of things, at the most awful period of life.

Some of the persons mentioned in these memoirs seem not to have been deeply impressed with re-

ligious considerations, till near the termination of
their days : they had then to lament the misapplication of their time, and the delay of the great
work for which they were brought into existence.
Others appear to have made an early, or more seasonable choice of virtue and goodness for their
portion ; and to have spent a great part of their
lives in the fear and love of God, and in doing good
to mankind. They enjoyed that peace of mind
which the world could neither give nor take away :
and a cheering well-grounded hope accompanied
them to the closing scene, that there was reserved
for them a crown of immortal honor. What an
evidence on behalf of piety and virtue ! What a
dissuasive from vice and folly ! And how animating to weary travellers to persevere in the paths
of goodness, and to keep their eyes fixed on that
happy country, where they too shall rest for ever
from all their labors !

But we live in a world of danger and temptation. Propensities to evil are powerful. The
riches, honors, and pleasures of life are continually
alluring us to an immoderate love and pursuit of
them. The subtle enemy of all good is perpetually on the watch, to avail himself of our weakness
and exposure, and to ensnare and destroy us. Our
safety, therefore, consists in being always on our
guard and in steadfastly resisting every approach
of evil.

But who is sufficient for these things ? In this

situation, how shall we preserve our innocence, maintain the warfare, and finally become victorious? There is not a more evident and important truth, than that the power of accomplishing these great ends of life, is not of ourselves. It proceeds from the grace of God; unto whom we are directed to apply daily, for preservation in temptation, and deliverance from evil.

The perusal of valuable books, reflection, conversation, and other means of moral and intellectual improvement, are indeed of great use and importance. Besides enlarging the mind, and promoting our temporal comfort and advantage, they may spread before us a pleasing view of the beauty and excellence of religion; and may occasion some desires for the possession of that happiness which it confers: but unless the DIVINE AID be sought for and superadded, they will not be able to produce that strength of resolution, and steady perseverance, which are necessary to crown our labors with success. Interest, passion, depraved inclination, and the love of the world, in constant operation, are too powerful to be controlled, by slight and temporary convictions of mind, or feeble and transient wishes of the heart.

May we, therefore, never rest satisfied with clear apprehensions of our duty, just sentiments of the beauty and excellence of Religion, and frequent desires to become its disciples, and to partake of its felicity! May we be earnestly and steadfastly concerned to apply, through the Redeemer of mankind, to the Giver of all good, for the assistance of his Holy Spirit, as the only power which can sanctify and render effectual our endeavors to please him, and produce in us the highest perfection of our nature!

He that formed our spirits, who is constantly present with us, and without whose superintendence not a sparrow falls to the ground, knows all our wants and frailties; and is not only able, but abundantly disposed, to grant all our humble and pious requests, and to give us every necessary support and comfort. "Ask, and it shall be given you; seek, and ye shall find; knock, and it shall be opened unto you." Let us not, therefore, be dismayed by the perils of our situation, whatever they may be, or by the feebleness of our powers. With humble confidence, let us implore the God of love and mercy, to forgive all our offences; to conduct us safely through the present life; and to prepare us for a happy immortality.

ALPHABETICAL INDEX.

A

B

C

D

E

G

H

I

J

L

M

N

O

P

R

S

RECOMMENDATIONS OF THIS WORK.

"WE have had frequent occasion to speak of the diligence, good sense, and good intentions, of Mr. Murray; and we congratulate him sincerely on the success of this particular work. We announce this edition, because the alterations and additions are so considerable, that it is rendered almost a new work."—*British Critic, July,* 1801.

" The examples which Mr. Murray has here selected, and the judicious reflections which accompany them, are such as can scarcely fail to make the best impressions, and to produce the best effects, on all who read them with attention. The present edition of this excellent publication, which has been long known and commended, is enlarged by the addition of twenty-two new characters, filling nearly one hundred pages."—*Anti-Jacobin Review, January,* 1804.

" We have received the *tenth* and last edition of this valuable work. The improvements made in it, will appear from the Author's *Advertisement.* We can only add to this account of the present useful volume, our hope that it will be extensively circulated among our countrymen."—*The American Review and Literary Journal, for July, August, and September,* 1801.

" On reviewing this book, in its improved form, we find the facts unquestionable and highly interesting—the style correct and neat—and the general tendency of the work such as induces us strongly to recommend it, especially to young readers; who love entertainment mingled with instruction."—*Evangelical Magazine, October,* 1801.

" The rapid sale of this small but valuable collection, has anticipated the commendation we are desirous to bestow. In an exemplification of more than *seventy* remarkable characters, many striking examples are exhibited, which, in the quiet hour of reflection, may contribute to arrest the careless and wandering; to animate the sincere and virtuous; and to convince or discountenance those who have been unhappily led to oppose the highest truths."—*Gentleman's Magazine, November,* 1803.

"In an age like the present, when Infidelity seems to have thrown away her mask, as no longer being ashamed to disclose her daring front;—when a laxity of morals prevails even among believers, and men stick not to insinuate that an indulgence in crimes expressly forbidden by our holy religion, will find excuse in the eye of that Being, who knows he formed us *frail creatures ;*—at such a season, it is of the highest importance, to recur to the piety of those comparatively few bright examples, who will be of singular efficacy to excite in us a love of God and goodness.

"Mr. Murray, with much commendable zeal, has, in the volume before us, provided the reader with an assemblage of virtuous and religious characters. The conduct of the greater part of them, at the approach of death, affords a lesson which all are concerned to learn—that 'the fear of the Lord' alone 'is wisdom,' and to depart from evil the only ' understanding.' "—*Critical Review, June*, 1803.

"This judicious biographical selection is already too well known, to stand in need of our recommendation ; but we nevertheless avail ourselves of a corrected and augmented edition, to add our approbation, to that which it has justly received from the most respectable classes of the public."—*Eclectic Review, April*, 1806.

"This work, which has been long and justly admired, has, in the last edition, received many alterations and improvements; and, in its present enlarged state, forms, in our opinion, one of the best books that can be put into the hands of young people." —*Guardian of Education, August*, 1803.

"That 'examples draw, where precepts fail,' is a truth which has been acknowledged in all ages and nations; and on the strength of this principle, Mr. Murray has had recourse to experience, in evincing the power and importance of religion. He has thus furnished an interesting collection of testimonies; and we wonder not, that a work so instructive and amusing, as well as impressive, should have been generally patronised. It is a book which may be read with profit, by persons in all situations; and with the rising generation, it may answer the double purpose, of improving them in biography and in virtue."—*Monthly Review, August*, 1801.

www.ingramcontent.com/pod-product-compliance
Lightning Source LLC
Chambersburg PA
CBHW021718110726
47902CB00005B/1241